THE
IDEA OF PERFECTION
IN THE
WESTERN WORLD

THE IDEA
OF PERFECTION
IN THE
WESTERN WORLD

By Martin Foss

UNIVERSITY OF NEBRASKA PRESS · LINCOLN

BD
233
F6

53491

TO MY WIFE

PREFACE

This book is a critique. A critique gains in strength when concentrated on one definite object, and it gains in importance when the chosen object stands for more than itself and permits expansion over a wider sphere of philosophical thought. I think that the object chosen is important enough to lead to a multitude of vital problems. These problems have received a more extended treatment in my *Symbol and Metaphor*, first published in 1949, and reissued as a paperback by the University of Nebraska Press in 1964.

The continuity of philosophical tradition is something I believe in. Therefore this book must follow the great and unbroken tradition of centuries. Those thinkers whose occasional statements are criticized in this work are not less a part of this great tradition. Their important contribution has never been doubted. In fact, I have learned most from those men whom I was compelled to criticize, and I wish to make it clear that my attack is—to use a famous word—nothing but a form of sincere gratitude.

CONTENTS

CONTENTS

THE
IDEA OF PERFECTION
IN THE
WESTERN WORLD

INTRODUCTION

ONE of the most fundamental, and perhaps one of the most crucial problems of philosophy is that of outlining its own tasks, limits, and possibilities. Born in the sphere of religious meditation and ethical conflicts, out of the urge to clarify and deepen our knowledge of human value and human devotion, philosophy soon turned to the field of inorganic nature and tried to give an image of the world independent of human evaluation and of the emotions of the soul. Democritus already experiences the breach of the two worlds: on the one hand he organizes science in his atomic system, in order to master the world by quantitative relations; on the other hand he is the first to cast light on the depth of the human soul and lays the ground for a significant and profound ethics. The atomic system, however, and ethics do not go together. Law and order, static mastery of the world of nature, systematic balance of thought become the ideals of Greek philosophy, and these ideals are handed down to the following generations for which quantitative relationship and mathematical science shape the view of the world.

As fascinating, however, as this view may be, and as stimulating as it has been for the development of civilization, philosophers have never felt entirely satisfied. In Christian time, particularly, the ethical and religious life pleaded its cause before the judgment of truth. And so the course of European philosophy is marked by a permanent struggle between a rational philosophy and a desire to understand the position of man in the universe. It is the religious thinker who in the Christian era revolts against a systematizing reason and tries over and over

3

again to break its power by violent paradoxes.[1] For it is the paradox which often in the history of philosophy stands as a storm-signal indicating the shortcomings of a current method, and so as a symptom of an inner disturbance may become the means of a recovery, if it is rightly understood. But it was not always rightly understood and so did not always lead to a new and more profound research of the truth. Sometimes, on the contrary, the course of philosophy has been shaped by an endeavor to escape new problems and the challenge of a spiritual crisis. Thinkers have tried to compromise and, by extending to all spheres of knowledge one and the same limited but exact scientific method, they have not so much solved problems as avoided problems which they despaired of solving. In this way philosophy has given up trying to understand ethics, aesthetics, and religion in their own fields and has made itself the handmaid of science. It has adopted the method of natural science and has systematically schematized the sphere of human values.

If philosophy wants to preserve its own unique task and if it wants to remain the link between the two realms of the inorganic world and the world of the living, then it must withdraw from its compromises. Even at the risk of being criticized, it is necessary for philosophy to correct and reduce to their true limits certain concepts which have their place in the field of practical systematization and technical work, but which have been hypostasized and have in vain attempted to explain the ulti-

[1] Tertullian: *De Carne Christi* 5: "certum est quia impossibile est"; Master Eckhart, Edit. Pfeiffer 206, 34: "If truth were understandable, it would not be true"; Cusanus, *De Docta Ignorantia* 1, 3: "The more we know that we do not know, the nearer we are to the truth."

mate foundation of our existence. Such a concept is the idea of the divine and human perfection.

There are not many concepts in the history of philosophy which have so great a significance as has the idea of perfection. There must have been good reason for the dominating position which this idea attained. It is always a mistake to undervalue a statement to which one is opposed. To do this means failure and, in the end, surrender to its unbroken power. So Spinoza attacked perfection as a mere prejudice and nevertheless fell under the spell of this same idea. "Men began to form universal ideas," he says,[2] "and so it happened that each person called a thing perfect which seemed to agree with the universal idea which he had formed of that thing." These "universal ideas" which Spinoza attacks as mere prejudices are by no means arbitrary. It may happen in our daily life that we form ideas without sufficient insight and that we sometimes give an answer before we have truly and rightly asked the question. We may be inclined to anticipate a truth which we investigate and prove, if ever, only post-festum. But these anticipations, these "pre-judices" are somehow necessary and important means to scientific thinking. Every theory, every law is just such a mental anticipation, and it is the task of scientific research to confirm it later on. Science here presupposes "universal ideas" and considers them as an anticipated perfection, in order to reach this perfection by a subsequent investigation of details. When Democritus proclaimed the theory of atoms he set a standard of perfect scientific truth, and the scholars in later centuries tried to verify this pattern of perfection by experiment and research. Surely scholars in modern times begin to

[2] Spinoza: *Ethics*, IV, Preface.

5

doubt whether these "universal ideas" really convey absolute perfection. They regard them merely as hypotheses, as provisional truths of limited significance, and even this restricted meaning of universal ideas has often raised the scorn of the conscientious scholar. When Newton declares: "Hypotheses non fingo," or when Goethe calls hypotheses lullabies which send the scholar to sleep, they revolt against the ultimate perfection of a "universal idea." Nevertheless, even a Newton had to "feign" hypotheses and every scholar has to do likewise. To form "universal ideas" is not a whim; it is the necessary method of scientific research, working under the ideal of total, complete, and perfect mastery of the material.

When we consider the fact that even in the field of science, where it is an important means of research, the ideal of perfection has been doubted and restricted to a hypothetical perfection, it is hardly understandable that in all other fields, in the fields of human value: in ethics, aesthetics and religion, this ideal stands its ground and has seldom been seriously contested. Even those philosophers who acknowledge only hypothetical laws in the scientific realm demand categorical, unconditioned perfection in the realm of life and action. Since Socrates made the good an absolute standard of perfection, the ethical systems of all following centuries have tried to give a more and more precise meaning to this standard of perfection. Is this endeavor justified? Or is it a delusion? And is it a destruction of all ethics and a deadly blow to the dignity of men, to doubt this endeavor? One might object that education loses its meaning without a standard of perfection, and that if the teacher does not have such a standard he will not be able to pass it on to his pupil. "And how," the defender of perfection may continue, "can we protect beauty and the arts against distintegration and against the skeptical view of those who regard these values as merely relative, if we do not acknowledge a perfect beauty? What the artist tries to convey in his work is perfection, and because it is perfection it moves us and lifts us up. It may even lead to a religious vision, because also in the sphere of religion it is perfection which we seek in God. Our human ethical perfection makes us into an image of God. God himself is perfection." Here, in God, all threads of thought seem to converge: Our moral endeavor, our artistic creation are both regarded as approaches to the perfection which we think is in God. The ideal of perfection has its highest fulfillment in theology and religious thought, and in this realm it seems unassailable. But in this very realm it is, as we shall try to point out, the least firmly established and, far from deepening the divine greatness in our hearts, it debases and reduces the sublimity of the divine. Therefore our study has to lay considerable emphasis on this point. Starting with a short explanation of the term "perfection," as it was used in the history of philosophy, we shall see that already in Greek thought the concept of perfection transcends its limits and inclines toward a hypostasis. And as we follow the course of history throughout the Christian era we shall observe a struggle of ideas which results in a compromise between the Greek hypostasis of perfection and the Christian idea of the living God. We will, however, have to investigate the ideal of perfection not only on religious ground: it will be our task also to challenge the dominating position which the idea of perfection has maintained in the realm of aesthetics and ethics until our modern time.

1

THE IDEA OF PERFECTION AND
GREEK PHILOSOPHY

I

WHAT is "perfection"? Let us set forth the problem as simply as possible. Perfection is the conformity of a reality to its concept. Wherever a thing is found adequate to the idea which we have of it that thing is perfect. It is obvious that such conformity of a thing to its concept will be most exact whenever the thing has been constructed after the model of the concept. Perfection, therefore, will occur most generally as the conformity of execution to purpose. Purpose, end is the essence of perfection. This was stated by Aristotle[1] and later by St. Thomas Aquinas. The latter gives as one of the definitions of perfection, the fitness to purpose.[2] And Kant stresses the relation between purpose and perfection in saying: Perfection is objective purposiveness.[3] Therefore: Perfection is an attribute of things. A thing, manufactured according to purpose, is perfect. The adaptation of the material to the form, the full realization of the idea which a man has in starting to work on a thing makes the finished object perfect.

We may use this literal sense of "perfection of deliberately manufactured things" in a figurative sense for persons. We will do this, however, only when these per-

[1] Aristotle: *Metaph.* 1021 b.

[2] Thomas Aquinas: *De Nom.* I, 3: "Perfectio consistit in hoc quod pertingat ad finem"; also *Summa Theol.* I qu. 6 a. 3; qu. 73 a. 1; *Contra Gent.* III, 16. God's Perfection as finality: *Summa Theol.* I qu. 1 a. 1; *Summa Theol.* I qu. 65 a. 2.

[3] Kant: *Critique of Judgment* § 15.

sons are more or less absorbed in a certain purpose. We may speak of a perfect butler, a perfect cook, a perfect physician. In society where men are usually objectified, classified according to their purposes, or according to their usefulness, the concept of perfection plays a great role. Society simplifies and abbreviates its members to executors of their social purposes, their social professions. This far and only this far they are evaluated, and if they are adequate to their purpose in the social scheme, they are called perfect. So we have perfect typists, perfect lawyers, perfect accountants. But are there also "perfect men"? I do not think so. But more about this later.

Every purpose is a limited one. It is even called an "end." It is essential for the purpose to be a termination. Certainly the purpose can find its place in a broader arrangement. But then it loses its character as an end and changes into a means for another end which again appears to be an ultimate object, a termination and limit.

In such a widened arrangement of purpose the means will have to be adequate to the end and ultimate aim, if the thing is to achieve perfection. All the means will have to be used, and will have to be adequate. The end as a perfect object has disposed of a totality of means, it is this totality. It is complete. It is limited as an end, but in this limitation complete.

And this complete limitation and seclusion we call absolute. Every end is—so to speak—absolute as an end. It has nothing besides itself, it is in all regards rounded up and walled up in itself. This fact is blurred in cases where human life is seen under the aspect of purpose and end. Surely a human being is never entirely absorbed in his purposes or profession; he may be perfect as a butler complete as such—but he is not only a butler. He is more

Only in regard to a limited sphere of his life we call him perfect and only in so far as we transform him into a useful object, an expedient thing do we feel an absolute satisfaction and fulfillment. But let us consider a machine; a power-loom of which the pistons and levers work without any friction does its weaving well and is, therefore, in all regards perfect—nobody would expect it to bake bread besides. It is an ultimate, absolute fulfillment of its concept, because it is the flawless realization of its one and only end.

The more limited an end is, the more we can expect perfection to be attained. Perfection, therefore, is something we come across in simple affairs, in daily life. When we behave very modestly and restrict ourselves to the most simple aims, we can be sure to produce perfections in large quantities. And to go back again to the analogy of human life: a man who is most onesided, restricted, and specialized in a very limited field will easily achieve perfection. What we accomplish by training in a restricted sphere—making it into a habit, into a kind of instinctive action—will always be perfect. It is the technical dexterity and skill which—concentrated on a small field—attains perfection. Kant indeed defines perfection plainly as dexterity and skill.[4] By training, habit, and specialization we reduce our human possibilities to a subhuman instinctive necessity which is perfect in its exactitude and surety. We find this dexterity still more in animals which execute their ends with an infallibility men can never achieve. We feel admiration and pleasure, for instance, in observing the perfect ease and sureness with which an ape climbs a tree.

[4] Kant: *Critique of Pract. Reason* § 8 Remark II.

10

In so far the animal really is and can be a model of perfection—it is not necessary to refer to God as the source of perfection in the mind of men. The proof of Descartes which bases the existence of God on our consciousness of perfection[5] is—to say the least—rather far-fetched. We may find perfection abundantly in our own life and even more abundantly in the life of animals.

Somebody, however, may raise the following objection: It is true that we find perfection in the most limited and inferior sphere, but there are different levels of perfection, lower and higher ones, and there is a highest perfection.

But that objection is not defensible. For, on the contrary, perfection is always perfection, i.e. conformity of a thing to its end. There are no degrees because perfection is always "perfect perfection." And there cannot be any comparison between perfections *qua* perfections. Certainly, one thing is more valuable than another, but not because of its perfection. Perfection is something which we presuppose and even omit, as self-understood, when we compare things. We always compare perfect samples of things, in order to find their differences of value. "Perfection" does not give us any clue as to the essence of a thing, but only to the way in which a thing represents—partly or fully—its species. When we hear that an engine is perfect, we do not know a thing about the engine itself; when we are told that somebody is a perfect butler, we do not learn anything about the functions of a butler. A perfect God would be a God who represents the divine qualities in a perfect way—whereby we would be left absolutely in the dark as to what these divine qualities are.

[5] Descartes: *Med.* III.

11

II

However, let us adopt, for the moment, the point of view that a perfection is a higher perfection when related to a higher activity. We will consider, therefore, the activity which may represent the highest achievement of men, that activity which lifts men above the animal: thinking. Our judging, inferring, abstracting, and systematizing is certainly a high human power. No wonder that men are proud of this their particular treasure, and that the Greeks who, so to speak, unearthed this treasure were enraptured by the splendor of spiritual accomplishment and the sublimity of the intellect. For them—and following them throughout the succeeding centuries—perfection meant the perfection of scientific systematization.

For the average man, of course, thinking goes on merely in the framework of his daily business. His aims are short, and the terms which serve his inferences are easily found. Perfection for him is the clarity and surety of judgment, the precision and accuracy of premises, and their conformity to the conclusion. We can state as a rule: the more simple and restricted the aim of thinking is, the easier perfection, i.e. perfect clarity, consistency, distinctness, and completeness can be achieved. Knowledge is always perfect, when related to a simple and limited field. Perfection is also here dexterity, sagacity, attainable by training and habit, and this training will aim at clarity, distinctness, completeness of concepts and their relation: the premises in relation to the conclusion, the predicates in relation to the subject, the applications in relation to the law. Clarity, distinctness, and completeness was the ideal of the Sophists, in order to convince and defeat their opponents, and their dexterity and training may sometimes have turned into a game. Their influence, however, was enormous; they organized schools and education, and from them the ideal of intellectual training was inherited by the philosophers of the Renaissance. Their ideal became the ideal of Descartes, whose philosophy—like that of the Sophists—was to a great extent methodology of clear and distinct thinking, perfection. Even Spinoza and Leibniz fell partly under the spell of Cartesian influence, and everywhere the result of this methodological dexterity was a glorification of the ideal of perfection. But everywhere the result was also mechanization, transformation of life into a system of fixed objects.

But now we come to a circumstance which caused the hypostasis of "perfection" in the field of thought and proved fatal to the religious development of the Western World: Our aims are limited. Their limitation, in fact, makes possible their completeness and perfection. Our concepts, too, are limited and in their limitation clear, distinct, and perfect. In life and action, however, we are forced to stop at the limits of our aims, but we are not forced to do so in the process of thought. In life the necessity of limitation may fall as a dark shadow on men, may give them the feeling of insufficiency, guilt, failure, and uselessness of striving. The Greeks felt it deeply and built their great tragedy around this essential experience. Because they felt more than others this tragedy of failure and restriction in life, they fled into the sphere of pure thought, where the aims can be extended to the highest degree. The more pure our thinking is and the less this thinking serves daily goals—where pragmatism tries to enclose it—the more the clarity and perfection of our concepts turns out to be merely the means to proceed to other concepts, to recognize the relativity of all perfect limitation and so to seek relation to innumerable other concepts. Every judgment and conclusion is well founded and perfect only in order to lead to other judgments. So the sphere of thought widens, concept links to concept, judgment to judgment, law to law—and this whole is based upon an optimistic conviction: the conviction of the existence of a concept which contains all other concepts, an order so wide and extensive that it embraces as a total order all possible orders. That this order—although total, indeed because total—nevertheless has to be limited, as every concept is total because limited, is the paradox of this holy conviction which bears the name of truth.

So the Greeks discovered a spiritual world, a world-order: the "cosmos" which is total and limited, a totality resting in equilibrium. It is a Greek ideal, even a Greek religion, and the God of this religion is the order of a satisfied cosmos, happy and appeased in its limits. The realization of this cosmos became for the Greek people their small city-state, limited, enclosed in its walls, and in its seclusion, perfect.

Had Greek thought ended here, it would have discovered—in the concept of spiritual perfection—science as a totality, as a system. This alone would have been a revolution in the development of mankind: mathematics, natural science, transformed into a system, perfected to a well-rounded whole—especially astronomy as the doctrine of circular motion in celestial bodies—would have manifested the closed, rounded, and limited totality as the highest meaning and goal of our knowledge, as a symbol of holy perfection. With all that, however, only the concept of science would have been discovered, not philosophy, not metaphysics. The conviction of the existence of an all-embracing concept did not seem enough. This concept had to be found.

14

Here, however, an insurmountable obstacle seems to rise. The wider the sphere of relations and the more the law of order and the conceptual entity expands, the less content there is. It is as if form grew at the expense of content, the subject at the expense of its predicates. It is as if gain in width is balanced by loss in intensity and concreteness. The early Greek philosophy touched only lightly on this problem and treated it with a certain ambiguity. Parmenides decreed simply that the most extensive concept had to be the most concrete, and concluded that the concept of BEING as coincident with thinking[6] is the fulfillment of the young metaphysical urge. This being is not only thinking, but also object of thinking, thought, form, and content.[7] This ambiguity, however, had a fatal consequence. Although Parmenides emphasized again and again that being is indivisible and one, a certain multitude and quantity entered into the indivisible being with the ambiguity of a subject which is also object, a form which is also content. Being is perfection and perfection is completeness. So the being of Parmenides assumes the character of "complete being," of "all." And with this concept of "all," the perfect universe and cosmos as a complete quantity arises.

The being of Parmenides is paradoxical. "All" is quantity, complete and perfect quantity, and cannot be the one and predicateless being. "All" means "all things," whereby the quality of these things is left indistinct. The indistinctness and ambiguity of the "all" allows it to combine with the likewise indistinct being and so to introduce completeness secretly and unconsciously as perfect quantity into being. Parmenides, therefore, cannot repeat often enough that being is all: "The being is as an

6 Diels: *Fragm. der Vorsocr.* 3rd Edit. page 152; Frag. 5.
7 Diels: *ibid.* page 157; Frag. 8.

all in the now," or "being is shut off at all sides," or "being is all-filled," or "being is all-coherent."[8]

The completeness and perfection of the all has another no less paradoxical consequence. Completeness, perfect totality is something finished, limited. Limit belongs to all, as all to limit,[9] and Parmenides calls being rightly "all-limited." "All" signifies "all possibilities serving a certain actuality"; "all" signifies "all means for a certain end," or "all predicates for a certain subject." Completeness as perfection is limited. Totality is limitation. It is therefore, a natural consequence that the "all" and "being" of Parmenides assume a limited form: the Globe,[10] and for most of the Greeks the cosmos, remained a globe.

The religion which corresponds to this ideal of perfect completeness is the sanctification of completeness, of totality and all: pantheism. Pantheism means that the all, because it is all, is divine. It is a contradictory divinity, limited, indistinct, and nevertheless perfect; one, but nevertheless quantity. Only by interpolating into this concept the idea of life can we grasp and feel the meaning of this strange deity in its ambiguous and paradoxical perfection.

With this metaphysical dogma, however, the idea of perfection begins to lose its meaning. Perfection was and could only be the conformity and completeness of means for the goal, or of predicates for the subject. A subject of which the predicates are not conceived—which even has no predicates and therefore cannot be in conformity to them—can only arbitrarily be called perfect. In fact "being" is a most imperfect and empty concept.

[8] Diels: *loc. cit.* pages 155, 156, 158.
[9] Aristotle: *Met.* 1022 a uses the concept "all" to explain the concept "limit."
[10] Diels: *loc. cit.* page 158.

The clarity and distinctness which is essential to all perfection has changed into utter unclarity and indistinctness. "Being" in its abstraction and onesidedness, as a purely intellectual scheme, is not even a working-hypothesis. It leads to nothing and it explains nothing. It is a totality which is limited, but which has nothing to limit it. "Nothing," this nothing develops now into the great danger of philosophy, its terror but at the same time its stimulus. From now on the problem of "nothing" shows an ever growing importance for the philosophy to come. It threatens and attracts, it repels and allures. The development of Greek philosophy is pushed forward by the "nothing" and its problems.

For Parmenides the "nothing" is unreal, a mere appearance and fiction. What, however, is appearance in contrast to essence? A merely fictitious "nothing" threatens to transform the limits of being into fictitious limits and so to make being flow into the infinite. Parmenides did not solve this problem which was a challenge to his notion of perfection. Neither did Socrates, who nevertheless felt the demonic influence of the nothing behind all his efficient optimism of conceptual constructions and perfect definitions; repeatedly he strikes against walls, which makes him confess his ultimate ignorance. Not until Plato was the problem of nothing seriously broached. Throughout Plato's long life the problem of "being" and "not being" was the driving force in his development. First of all, the multitude of the ideas was a breach in the original perfection of the one and total being, and never did Plato make it quite clear whether this multitude is comprised in a unity of the good, of proportion—or whether there is no embracing unity at all. Far more important, however, in this connection, is another problem, that of "becoming." Becoming is now the place where the "nothing" enters the "being"; it is being and nothing together, and the fact that "nothing" can be so closely connected with "being" is a new and somewhat alarming item in the Platonic system, which brings it near the paradoxical thought of Heraclitus. It is true that Plato states that the process of becoming is merely appearance compared to the pure being of the ideas. But in the course of his development the appearance of becoming achieves more and more importance. The nothing is now perceived in its close relation to being as the "different,"[11] and is at last clarified by Aristotle's crystal thinking into the concept of "potentiality," of "matter" as the source of actuality.[12]

And from this time on matter absorbs a great part of the problems involved in the concept of "nothingness." Matter is now the dark, alluring, and at the same time repelling, sphere of reason. What is matter? While before it was nothingness which threatened perfection, now it is matter, which is a strange element in the perfect world of intellectual completeness. In one of the most ingenious endeavors in the history of philosophy, Aristotle tries to solve the problem and to save the idea of absolute perfection. He does it by creating his concept of "entelechy." The process of becoming, this unstable stream of change —always in danger of vanishing into the unlimited, the infinite—is caught again in boundaries: in the concept of an end, of "telos." Becoming is the realization of this its end which was also its beginning. All becoming turns out to be a limited and static circular movement of "final cause." Matter is only the way to form; and it is unreal with regard to the fact that form was already there before the way began.

[11] Plato: *Sophistes* 257.
[12] Aristotle: *Met.* 1033 a.

Aristotle cannot, however, carry this thought through to its ultimate consequence. Matter assumes in Aristotle's system an ever growing importance, beyond appearance and fiction. Development of form is an indubitable reality. The world of matter exists, and Aristotle follows its development with the love and passion of the discoverer. Perfection is in danger of becoming an attribute of all limited beings, as their essence, their meaning and end: a very limited, a very profane, very modest perfection. Here, however, Aristotle breaks away from the clear line of thought. In order to save the idea of the one and absolute perfection he constructs a new paradox, the paradox of the aim which aims at itself; the form which is its own content; the thinking which is its own thought. This highest entelechy, in which the ideas of end, of form, content, even of thought, cancel themselves, is God. God as the aim which aims at itself, the thought which thinks itself and nothing but itself, is the salvation of the one and absolute perfection.

So Aristotle, as the first Scholastic, is in a position to formulate the first real proof of the existence of God, and he bases this proof naturally on the concept of perfection.[13] And in starting with the paradox of an absolute self-aim—an end which is its own realization, a form which absorbs its content—he comes to the statement that development on the whole consists in an ever growing absorption of content by form, an ever growing realiza-

[13] Aristotle: "On Philosophy" in *Fragmenta* (Editio Teubneri) Frag. 16. Plato's proof of God in *Laws* x cannot be considered as a real proof, since Plato does not make it clear whether there is one God or as many Gods as there are souls. It is interesting to see, by the way, that even Aristotle in his later years did not adhere strictly to the one perfect God, but was compelled to suggest 47 (55) different Gods; perfection as limited end does not seem to agree with the oneness of God. (see *Metaph.* chap. 8 of book XII, a late interpolation).

tion of pure form. Reality is form and the degrees of development are degrees of reality, degrees of intellectual truth. Pure thought is pure reality and as such it is pure perfection. In this way reality and perfection become synonymous as they occur later on in the philosophy of Thomas Aquinas and Spinoza, and they can become synonymous because thought alone exhausts the whole sphere of reality. It is the highest triumph of the rational idea of end. Only the reasonable exists, says Hegel, and so he repeats the old dogma of Aristotelian perfection. Hegelianism is the most outstanding achievement of the Greek idea of finality, and although Hegel emphasizes that "perfection is an indeterminate idea,"[14] he has in fact adopted and restored the old Aristotelian idea of perfection as the circular movement of self-aim: His "absolute spirit" is the God of Aristotle, who only thinks himself, and his development is—according to Hegel's own statement—nothing but a circle, a return to the start.[15]

The idea of divine perfection has been bought at a high price. To save this idea, thought had to negate itself by becoming self-thought, end had to cancel itself as an aim which aims at itself; the creative movement was reduced to a static circle. Such a circle is something empty, useless and even meaningless. And empty and meaningless, therefore, is the idea of divine perfection.

Furthermore, this aim which aims at itself, which is its own content, assumes like every intended content the character of an object, a thing. God is in all philosophies of perfection a mere thing. Perhaps he is a thing which has made itself, but in any case he is a thing. This result did not disturb the Greeks; their divine cosmos was in-

[14] Hegel: *Philos. of Religion* III, B (ontological proof).
[15] Hegel: *History of Philos.* Introd. 2 b end.

deed an objective order which satisfied their imagination even though it was an object. The world of the pantheistic Greeks is an animated object. Their "nous" and their "logos" are often interpreted in a personal way, but Anaxagoras saw in his nous an objective world-soul and the logos of Heraclitus and his followers was an objective order, a law.

It is not to be wondered at that Christian philosophy also made God into an object, into a thing, whenever it adopted the Greek ideal of perfection. Anselm's famous proof of God's existence—based on perfection—calls God: "*id* quo mai*us* cogitari nequit,"[16] and Thomas Aquinas proves God the perfect God in referring to the different degrees of perfection in things.[17] God is the most perfect thing. For his follower Descartes, therefore, there is nothing but objects, and we see here how the philosophy of mechanism grows necessarily out of the Greek ideal of completeness and perfection. Man is "res cogitans" and God is an infinite "res cogitans." Spinoza is quite consistent in making God an objective substance. Perfection, as equal to reality, is in his philosophy the clear, intelligent, distinct, and complete systematization of things in a Cartesian world-mechanism. Also the characterization of God as highest good, as "summum bonum" has its origin here: "summum bonum" is the last content of purpose, the ultimate end, a highly desired object.

This transformation of God into an object is a rationalization and scientification of God. God is here nothing else but the scientific system in hypostasis, the order of abstract finalism. And like every order he needs a supplement in something which is to be set in order. If he does not confine himself to set himself in order, as the Aris-

16 Anselm: *Proslog.* 2.
17 Thomas Aquinas: *Summa Theol.* I qu. 2 a. 3.

totelian God does, he must find something besides and outside, on which to apply his order. And so we have in all these systems of perfection—beginning with the Greek —that dualism of a spiritual order on the one hand and of a material world on the other. And the perfection which concerns solely the spiritual order can scarcely be brought into relation to the world existing somehow apart from it. In fact, the perfect divine order, being in itself walled up and totally self-sufficient, cannot have any relation to this world. So Aristotle indeed denies any action of God in regard to the world; merely the love of the world toward him constitutes a kind of one-sided relation without any influence on God at all. In this same way Aquinas denies every real relation of God to the world.[18] All this is indeed a very complicated and scarcely understandable construction which renders God's perfection questionable and makes it seriously difficult to consider the problem of creation.[19]

The ideal of divine perfection is therefore imperfect. It exists exclusively and one-sidedly in the intellectual sphere, and it leaves the world to itself. It is pure abstraction, omission, and therefore defective. It is also paradoxical. It attempts to achieve with the totality of relations something which is beyond this totality: absoluteness. But totality in its limitation is never absolute.[20] It is merely exclusive. The cosmos, rightly understood,

[18] Aquinas: *Summa Theol.* I qu. 13 a. 7: "Cum igitur Deus sit extra totum ordinem creaturae et omnes creaturae ordinentur ad ipsum, et non e converso, manifestum est, quod creaturae realiter referuntur ad ipsum Deum, sed in Deo non est aliqua realis relatio eius ad creaturas, sed secundum rationem tantum inquantum creaturae referuntur ad ipsum," see also *Summa contra Gent.* II, 12.

[19] Creation according to Aquinas is without change and motion and is eternal as a divine action, while its effects are not eternal. (*Gent.* II, 17 and 35).

[20] On the difference between totality and absoluteness see page 33.

allows other total cosmoi, a multitude of worlds. Aristotle, however, demands exclusiveness in the sense of
absoluteness regarding his God. This combination of
total relation with absoluteness is not attainable except
in one way: as the relation which is, so to speak, the
negation of relation, making the sides of the relation
coincide and so contradicting the principle of relation
itself: identity. Identity is a relation which does not
relate anything, because it moves in a circle within itself.
In this relation which is no relation, but only appears as
if it were, the ideal of absolute totality is achieved. And
so it happens that throughout the history of philosophy,
and to a high degree in Greek thought, speculation flows
into identity, in order to achieve a kind of outward perfection and completeness. What in Parmenides' thought
was an ambiguous and very problematic urge to combine
being and thinking, subject and object, form of oneness
and content of "all" is now answered, clarified, and sys-
tematized into a logical and metaphysical principle: the
principle of identity. And so Aristotle can state clearly
that form and content, aim and object of aim, are identical and that this identity is God.

This identity, however, as a metaphysical principle
Aristotle keeps away from the world of matter, from the
concrete world of things and he adapts it merely to the
abstract realm of pure thought. Only in this field of
thought is subject identical with object, form with content. Only here the divine perfection is absolute. His followers, however, cannot bear these restrictions of the
divine, and slowly but irresistibly the principle of identity conquers the world of matter. Stoicism already inclines to identify spirit and matter and in Christian philosophy—under the spell of the Greek ideal of perfection
—the frenzy of identity knows no limits and mounts to

its highest peak: in God all is identical, all perfections
are one (Aquinas, Descartes), essence and existence
(Anselm,[21] Aquinas, Descartes), the possible and the
actual (Cusanus), the positive and the negative, God and
the world (Scotus, Cusanus).[22] Spinoza's intellectual love
of God toward himself is no less a symbol of identity[23]
than Kant's concept of positive freedom, where lawgiver
and lawtaker are identical. Kant's great disciple, Schelling, at last bases his whole system of metaphysics on the
idea of identity, which he also calls indifference.[24] Indifference, or zero, is the last consequence of the frenzy of
identity, and so zero is the last word which the intellect
has to say, after it has turned self-sufficient through the
idea of total perfection.

[21] In Anselm's famous proof of God's existence the Parmenidean ambiguity between existence and thought is repeated. Anselm takes the
"existence" of the concept God in our human mind for a sufficient
foundation on which to base the existence of God outside of our mind.

[22] As the sides of the relation of identity are indifferent to each other,
an indifference which makes it possible to exchange the one for the
other, it is not of great importance in these systems whether God is
understood to be a negation while the world is positive (Dionysios), or
whether God is positive and the world is a negation (Spinoza; determi-
natio est negatio); whether God is free possibility in regard to the world,
which is bound to necessity (teleological view, Leibniz), or whether God
is law and necessity in a contingent World (Spinozism, divine causality).
Although these theories seem in strict opposition to each other, they are
exchangeable, because they are based on the metaphysical principle of
identity.

[23] Spinoza's *Ethics* begins and is founded on a conglomeration of iden-
tities: "Causa sui" is "id cuius essentia involvit existentiam." This
means: The identity of cause and effect is identical with the identity of
essence and existence.

[24] Schelling's *Sämmt. Werke* I, IV, 115.

2

CHRISTIAN PHILOSOPHY AND ITS COMPROMISE WITH THE IDEA OF PERFECTION

I

THE idea of perfection is the basic idea of scientific systematization. No wonder that the scientific and systematic experiment to transform God into an intellectual entity and so to prove his existence logically has been based on the idea of perfection. Perfection is behind all these proofs. This is correct not only with regard to the cosmological proof which is clearly based on the idea of end, but quite so also with regard to the ontological proof. Taking existence as a predicate which is necessary to the perfect completeness of God, this proof states the identity of essence and existence in God and has no trouble in deducing from this presupposition that God necessarily exists.

The Jewish-Christian God of religion is far from the God of proofs, from the God of identity of essence and existence, from the thought which thinks itself, from the perfect thing and summum bonum. The God of the Bible has alarmingly little to do with the God of the philosophers. This alone would not justify the conclusion that there is something wrong in the concept of the philosophers. There also could be something wrong in our religious conception of God, as compared with the clarified philosophical concept. The infallibility of the philosophical concept, however, is strongly contradicted by its own inconsistency, its paradoxical character, and its one-sidedness. Furthermore, our religious conviction, which by no means should be undervaluated, disagrees thoroughly with it. We shall also see later on how, so to speak, secretly and under cover philosophy tries to get rid of the fetters which the restricted concept of Greek thought has put on the religious conviction.

When we consider without prejudice the concept of a "perfect God," we see that this concept is not only unsatisfactory but indeed very inadequate. A perfect God, a God who in a perfect way fulfills his end, is an irreligious concept. God is here transformed into a thing, into a lifeless but expedient and therefore perfect object.

An examination of the Old Testament shows that God bears a multitude of names but never the attribute of the "perfect God." He is the Lord, the unique God, the living God, etc. The word which the Old Testament uses in its most sublime passages, and which better than any other expresses the innermost nature of Jehovah, is the Hebrew word "kabod" which means: force, will, heart, or soul, and which appears in all parts of the Testament, in Prophets and Psalms. The force of God, the will of God is the dynamic, inward character of this religiousness. It is the creative principle that—like all creation—at one time destroys, because destruction of the old is the condition of the coming of the new, and at another time builds up and shapes with loving power the miracle of birth. It is an irrational principle because force as concept rejects every rational classification. The word "force" is a very indistinct and imperfect expression for something which we cannot grasp with our intellect, but which as our will lives in us and comes into our consciousness in the life of action. It is the creative force of God, of which the world is full,[1] of which the heavens

[1] Num. 14: 21 and Is. 6: 3.

26

are witness,[2] and which is raised above all the world.[3] This sublime force resides on the Mount Sinai[4] and appears now in tender kindness,[5] now as a severe force of punishment,[6] destroying the company of Korah.[7]

The Greek inheritance of the philosophers made it difficult for them to penetrate into the heart of this religiousness and they tried to replace it by the old ideal of a static and purely intellectual perfection. It is interesting in this context, and enlightening, to see what the translators of the Bible into Greek, the men of the Septuaginta, have done to the divine idea of force, of will and heart. They have rendered this concept of "kabod" very harmless by translating it into the word "doxa," i.e. into "opinion," "credit," "prestige." They have transformed the most inward principle of creation into an outward reflection, into a reflection upon the minds of the people who, impressed by the effects of this force, try to explain their impression intellectually. God's force exists for them only in so far as men have an opinion, a "doxa," of it, only in so far as it is observed and valued as "prestige." It is astonishing how little, even in Hellenistic time, the idea of an inner life and of a creative personality was understood.

The translators of the Bible, who in their turn had to use the Septuaginta, were in doubt what to make of the word "doxa." Their solution was the term "honor of God" or "glory of God." We have become accustomed to these terms throughout the centuries, they are sanctified by tradition, we associate with them what we feel to be God. And we therefore no longer see how inadequate these wrong translations are. They all draw God down to

2 Ps. 19: 1.
3 Ps. 57: 5.
4 Exod. 24: 16 and 40: 35.
5 Exod. 33: 18.
6 Num. 14: 10.
7 Num. 16: 19.

an inferior level. How can we speak of God's honor? Honor is the opinion which society has of its members. Also glory is only the outward reflection of our actions on society. All this indeed is "doxa"; it is a most superficial way even to judge men and utterly meaningless when applied to God.[8]

It was St. Paul who gave a new meaning to the inadequate "doxa," changing it into a principle more congenial to the Biblical spirit: it is the beautiful conception of the conquering power over suffering, the power of justification and salvation, which doxa signifies now.[9] This transformation of a term shows the struggle between Greek thought and Biblical spirit.

And in the same way as the Greek idea of doxa, the Greek concept of perfection also infiltrates the Biblical Scriptures. While the Old Testament never calls God a perfect God, but mentions as perfect only his ways or his law—and even this very rarely[10]—the New Testament under Greek influence uses "perfection" frequently and as an attribute of the divine Person. The best known and the most significant passage is the famous dictum in the Sermon on the Mount (Mat. 5: 48):[11] "Be you therefore perfect, even as your Father which is in heaven, is perfect." Who reads these words without prejudice will feel a certain dissatisfaction. What does "perfect" mean here? What can it mean to men, that they are admonished to be

[8] Sometimes the translation of kabod as doxa or glory or honor does not give any sense at all; so in Ps. 30: 12 and 57: 8 and 108 beg., where concerning men it means obviously soul, person, heart. See Kittel: *Herrlichkeit Gottes.*

[9] Rom. 8: 17; II Cor. 3: 10 and 18; 4: 4 and 17.

[10] II Sam. 22: 31; Ps. 18: 30; 19: 7; Deut. 32: 4.

[11] See also: Rom. 12: 2. Christ's perfection: Hebr. 2: 10; 5: 9; 7: 28. Perf. of saints: Col. 4: 12 ("perfect and complete"); James 1: 4 ("perfect and entire"); I Ep. St. John 4: 18 ("perfect love"); Col. 3: 14 ("charity as bond of perfection"); Phil. 3: 12 and 15.

absolutely perfect and to live the perfection of God? And this dissatisfaction grows by considering the context in which these words stand and for which they are a summary: Christ puts before men the sublime request to love their enemies, the most extraordinary request of Christian religion, an overflowing over all boundaries, an excess of love. And just this extreme, this most irrational demand is characterized by the frigid symbol of intellectual balance and order. A comparison with the same dictum in Luke (6: 36) makes it entirely clear that the redactor of the passage in Matthew has chosen an odd expression. Here the passage reads: "Be you therefore merciful, as your Father also is merciful." This indeed is full of meaning and is the adequate summary and conclusion of a demand to love one's enemies: charity, not perfection.

II

It is by no means accidental that the Jewish philosophers, whose adoration of the old God was stronger than the strongest Greek influence, very seldom surrendered to the ideal of divine perfection. Philo,[12] the first of them, emphasizes that God is beyond knowledge and beyond perfection. The same may be said of Maimonides,[13] and others. With a certain ardor these men refuse altogether the intellectual knowledge of God and the ideal of divine perfection which is a symbol of intellectual interpretation. Of course, the Jewish philosophers are not the only ones. We find similar currents of thought in Gnosticism and Neoplatonism, perhaps under the influence of Philo, and perhaps even as a development of the irrational

12 Philo: *De opif. mundi* 2, 8.
13 Maimonides: *More Nebuchim* I, 59.

trend in Plato and Aristotle.[14] So Plotinus' hierarchy of knowledge surpasses perfection and enters a sphere where perfection loses its meaning.[15] In the system of Dionysios Areopagita[16] and of Scotus Eriugena[17] also, God is beyond perfection.

These divinations however are only a beginning. The Christian philosophy pushes forward to new problems and unconsciously tries to break the exclusive authority of the old ideal of perfection. It is characteristic that the word "perfection" is preserved although it loses or changes its meaning.

Perfection meant an absolute completion, a finishing in its form and boundaries, a rounding off and termination. But now it assumes the signification of EXCELLENCE, i.e. of something which surpasses, excels—something "more than." It becomes a comparative, entering into a comparison with something else. To excel means to prove more than others. So perfection as excellence adopts a relative character; the perfect is perfect in relation to that which is imperfect, because it is the more in regard to the less. This comparative use of the term "perfection" is by no means justifiable; it is simply an old word used for a new meaning, for which it is not suitable. And this new meaning is an endeavor to break out of the empty circle of identical totality.—Furthermore, the comparative perfection develops into a superlative, and this in a rather violent way: perfect is now that relative to which a comparative cannot be perceived. The negation here is ex-

[14] Plato however disguises this irrational trend as he admits in Letter VII and as the mythological passages show; and Aristotle banishes it into the sphere of pure religion. (See *Fragmenta* Nr. 49 and 15.)

[15] Plotinus: *Ennead.* V, 3, 14 and VI, 9, 6.

[16] Dionysios: *De Divin. Nom.* II, 3; but chap. XIII shows the ambiguous use of "perfection."

[17] Scotus: *De Divis. Nat.* I, 14 seq.

tremely suspicious. To define the "perfect" in a negative
way means the most shocking offence against the ideal
of perfection. And what does it mean that "more cannot
be perceived?" By whom? By men. So perfection is now
the limit of human and rational capacity. It is still a
relative perfection, because it is related to the human
intellect. And the fact that its definition can only be
given by negation proves that although it means to be a
rational concept, it surpasses reason and moves into a
sphere beyond.

What we tried here to derive and investigate is
Anselm's concept of perfection, on which he bases his
famous proof of God's existence.[18] His idea of divine
perfection is a very strange one; it lies on the way from
less to more and is a relative perfection, relative to the
human mind. And here may be mentioned another relative perfection which is a certain improvement, because
it does not relate God's perfection to the human mind
but to God himself. I mean the idea that God surpasses
permanently his own perfection, that every stage of God's
perfection is perfect in relation to his previous stage.
This notion of divine "perfectibility" surely grew out of
the desire to bring the philosophical concept of perfection into greater conformity to the "living God" of the
Bible. But what does it really mean? If the meaning of
perfectibility is only the assertion that perfection has to
be achieved in phases, stages, in a development, of which
we can distinguish the various degrees—then we have
here a mere substitution of the way the human intellect
works, for the indivisible nature of God. It is the Hege-
lian way to observe the "absolute spirit" in its stages of

---

[18] Anselm: *Proslog.* 2: "Id quo maius cogitari nequit." See also Augustine: *De Doct. Christ.* I, 7: "aliquid quo nihil melius sit." Here Augustine states the "excellentia Dei."

development; the stages of God are at the same time the stages of our human knowledge. Apart from the audacious enterprise to identify the divine spirit with our human mind—behind this "perfectibility" is the old static idol of "perfection," with the only difference that the circle from start to end is not yet closed, although theoretically and in principle it has to be conceived as a closed one. We observe God and he observes himself as partly finished, on the way to the finish—on the way which has and must have an absolute limit and end. The absolute spirit of Hegel—although developing in perfectibility—must therefore earlier or later arrive at this end—and then "perfectibility" turns out to be the "complete perfection."

Or: perfectibility means a never ending excelling movement. Here, however, we have to ask: which meaning can the "more" or the "better" have in this excelling movement, when it cannot be measured by a last end? There must be a standard of surpassing, an ideal of perfection.[19]

After all, the concept of perfection, with the changes it underwent, is a compromise, but a very interesting compromise, because it is the way to a new truth.

And this way to a new truth has now to be followed: We use "perfection" and "excellence" synonymously because we are not aware any more that perfection is a static completeness and that excellence is a dynamic

[19] It is this concept of relative perfection and perfectibility which Prof. Hartshorne develops in his book *Man's Vision of God*. The self-surpassing God is one of the main themes of this interesting modern attempt to preserve, and at the same time to change and correct, the ancient concept of a total perfection which does not fit any more into our religious world.

movement beyond a limit. Perfection emphasizes the end, excellence the way. And so we do not become aware of the difference between the totality of conditions on the one hand, and the unconditioned on the other, the totality of parts as a "whole" on the one hand, and the "indivisible" on the other. We are in the sphere of an unconsciously growing development, and those who develop generally do not recognize the new that they are shaping.

The idea of the "ALL," of the totality of conditions is a fundamental concept of Greek thought and closely related to the idea of complete perfection. We found this all as a limited unity, symbolized in the globe.[20] The totality of conditions as "all" belongs, therefore, to the realm of conditions. It is even the highest fulfillment of this realm, its last and ultimate goal, an entirely immanent conception.

This is, however, by no means so with regard to the new concept into which totality, "all" now is transformed: the concept of the "UNCONDITIONED." The unconditioned in contrast to the totality of conditions is not the fulfillment of the conditional sphere. On the contrary, it denies and repels the whole category of condition, and transcends it. There is suddenly a "beyond." Here is the same drive "beyond" which we observed in perfection as excellence. In the concept of "excelling" there is, however, a comparison, a certain bond which ties the excelling to the excelled, while in the concept of the "unconditioned" there is an entire detachment, a digression into a newly discovered sphere. This detachment, in Latin the ABSOLUTE, is important in Christian philosophy. To be sure, a certain divination of it is to be found in Plato and

[20] Page 16.

33

Aristotle.[21] The concept of absoluteness, however, does not play the decisive role which it assumes in the later centuries. The development is slow and even in our time Christian philosophy does not always distinguish strictly between totality and absoluteness. We often hear people speak of "absolute totality," "unconditioned totality,"[22] although this is incorrect: The totality of conditions is in relation to its constituent conditions, it is a quantity and as all quantity it is relative. The absolute, however, is not a relation, there is no relative absoluteness.[23] And there is no "absolute relation," except the strange relation of identity which is an endeavor to unite relation and absoluteness. Identity, indeed, is the point of irruption of the absolute into Greek philosophy, and lives here in the Aristotelian concept of the divine entelechy which is an identity of form and content.[24]

The resistance against the absolute and the relapse into the Greek complete and perfect all is shown best by the undiminished power of the concept "omnipotence" and "omniscience" (total power and total knowledge). Even today philosophers and theologians attribute these qualities to God. If it is true, however, as we tried to show above, that "all" is a limited quantity, then it means a degradation for the Divine to be restricted to power and knowledge of merely "all." The God of the spherical cosmos knew and acted only with regard to his total globe and so he knew and did all and nothing else but all that

[21] Plato: *Sophistes* 255 c. Aristotle: *Met.* 1022 a; here the καθ'αὐτὸ is even called κεχωρισμένον, the separate, the absolute.

[22] So even Kant: *Critique of Pure Reason* (chap. Transcendent ideas).

[23] Descartes, however, speaks of a relative absoluteness, stating that some things are more absolute than others (*Rules for Direction of the Mind* vi). But see Leibniz: *Nouv. Ess.* ii, 17: "L'absolu est antérieur à toute composition et n'est point formé par l'addition des parties."

[24] Pages 18 and 23.

which concerned this globe. The living God of the Bible, however, the God of Creation, would not have created, had he known merely "all" and had he possessed power merely with regard to "all." The new which is essential for creation contradicts the Greek ideal of the limited total quantity.[25] The absolute God is not a "total" God, not a pantheistic God, not a perfect God. He is beyond all these relations. He therefore is not exclusive merely to other Gods and other worlds. The concept of the absolute as beyond all totality gave way to the Christian concept of divine transcendence.

The same clear and decisive distinction which had to be made between totality and the absolute now becomes necessary, too, with regard to the "whole" on the one hand and the "INDIVISIBLE" on the other. The concept of the whole is, like the "all," a concept of completeness and perfection. "All" is a quantitative completeness, while the "whole" is a qualitative completeness; it is an all, in which the quantity is arranged in a certain order, as a whole of parts.[26] It is a unity of parts, it may even be called "one," a one of parts. And the idea of the "one" is powerful in Greek philosophy. But the passionate and ecstatic rapture, with which the idea of the "indivisible one" fills the heart of men like Plotinus[27] shows that

[25] Kant: (*Critique of Pure Reason, Cosmol. Ideas,* I Part: Antinom.) constantly uses "totality of conditions" and "the unconditioned" as synonyms and so in fact has to face the cosmological antinomies. These antinomies reveal indeed the mistake which results from confusing the totality of conditions and the unconditioned, the absolute; and this mistake may have been committed by a great number of philosophers. The antinomies therefore disappear, when totality and the absolute are properly distinguished, as Kant does finally with regard to the problem of freedom and God. Freedom is not identical with the "totality" of causal determination; and God as substance and ground is not identical with the "totality" of inherent accidents.

[26] Aristotle: *Met.* 1024 a.   [27] Plotinus: *Ennead.* VI, 9, 6.

something entirely new is on the way. The "one" of the Greek philosophers is always a "whole," ἐν καὶ πᾶν or ἐν καὶ ὅλον, and a whole is a whole of parts, even if one refuses to divide it. The whole belongs in the category of parts and divisibility; there is reciprocity between whole and parts. Not only do the parts depend on the whole, but also the whole depends on the parts, for it is only a whole through the parts, and conditioned by the parts. Therefore, the Greek atom is a whole and a part. It is a whole and so has extension, weight, all the qualities which make a division possible; and it is a part which builds a whole together with other atoms, although this whole of atoms may flow in a wider whole of infinite emptiness. It may be called a last part, because it actually is not divided[28]—and this alone means: atom—but a last part does not stop being a part, and as such belongs in the category of parts and whole, of divisibility.

Quite different is the "indivisible" as that which is not only actually undivided, but essentially beyond the sphere of division, of part and whole. We may call it in distinction from the atom the "INDIVIDUAL." The individual transcends the category of whole and part, it is unrelated, not comparable to others, absolute, unique. With the new concept of true indivisibility men learn to know individuality and so they form the concept of God not only as the "one," but as the "unique God," the "individual God." This individuality of God is a perfection which has little in common with the old idea of the complete whole.

Aristotle already distinguishes between the actual individual substance and the ground of possible accidents

[28] Epicurus's atoms were even no last parts but composed of "minima."

which he calls matter.[29] But it was left to the Franciscan
philosophy, the philosophy of Duns Scotus and his followers, to emphasize the uniqueness of the individual.
While Thomism tried to explain individuality as a mere
quantitative difference,[30] Scotus stated the uniqueness
and incomparability of the individual. It is the indivisible "Haecceitas" which is discovered here and which
represents a higher reality than the genera and species,
an "ultima realitas entis."[31]

This new idea, however, is carried through very slowly.
Again and again philosophers fall back on the old concept of total perfection. When Descartes calls God perfect, because nothing "can be added,"[32] he moves in the
sphere of completeness and, with regard to our problem,
does not seem to be the instigator of a new philosophical
era but rather the end of an old one. In contrast with
him, Leibniz bases the ingenious concept of the mon-
adology on the idea of the individual, its uniqueness and
indivisibility. But his philosophy also is inclined to
compromise with the past. In degrading his monads to
parts of a whole he contradicts their uniqueness and
incomparability, and although denying the possibility
of empty space, his system of monads, like that of Epicurus's atoms, seems to flow in an empty infinity.

With the discovery of the absolute and the unique
individual a new problem arises, a problem of attitude
toward the uniqueness and absolute. The God of a relative order, of a lawful totality, the God of thought could

---

[29] Aristotle: *Metaph.* 1028 a 30; 1030 a 20; 1027 a 13; *Cat.* 5, 2 a and
5, 4 a.
[30] Aquinas: *Summa contra Gent.* II, 49.
[31] Duns Scotus: *Op. Oxon. dist.* III qu. 2 n. 15. Spinoza takes a very
definite stand with regard to this problem: every individual encloses
God's eternal and infinite essence. (*Ethics* II Propos. 45.)
[32] Descartes: *Medit.* III.

be approached by the mediation of inference and rational proof. This God could be known, just as cosmos, completeness, totality, perfection are known. But how to approach the unique, absolute God? A relation to the absolute is paradoxical. And so the absolute God indeed was often transformed into a relative God, related to the human intellect, as was done by Anselm[33] and others. Another approach, however, is now needed; an immediate approach, and this immediate approach is what we call "intuition."[34] We find this approach already in Plotinus' attitude toward the "indivisible one." We find something similar in the Platonic and Aristotelian religious philosophy, based on the relation of identity, the "absolute relation," as a compromise between relativity and absoluteness. Whenever in the following centuries men feel inclined to compromise between the Greek and the Christian ideal, the identifying intuition becomes the essential means of knowledge. It is the identical in us which sees the identical outside of us, as Empedocles[35] states and as Plato[36] describes it in his famous dictum of our sunlike eye which makes us see the sun. It is the divine in us which makes us know the Divinity and so this identifying intuition runs through Christian mysticism, where man identifies himself with his God. This is a Greek inheritance and is later on replaced by an attitude more adequate to the Christian idea of the Divine.[37]

[33] See page 31.

[34] Duns Scotus: *Report. Paris.* IV dist. xlix qu. 7 n. 4.

[35] Diels: *loc. cit.* page 262 *Empedocles Fragm.* 109.

[36] Plato: *Rep.* 508 and Plotinus: *Ennead.* I, 6, 9. Plato (Letter VII 344 a) bases knowledge on συγγένεια, i.e. kinship between knower and known.

[37] The identifying intuition had a strong revival in the field of ethics and aesthetics during the nineteenth century under the name of "einfuehlung." Man's knowledge of man seemed to be based on the identity

The ideal of totality, completeness, and perfection was, as we saw over and over again, closely related to the idea of limitation. In the realm of the absolute, of the individual, however, totality and limitation do not hold. A new and powerful concept springs up—the concept of INFINITY. Infinity, indeed, is one of the fundamental concepts of the Christian philosophy, and in order to grow into this central position it undergoes decisive changes and assumes an absolutely new character. For most of the Greek philosophers the infinite is chaos, the dark sphere of disorder and emptiness. It is the imperfect which either does not exist at all, or exists only as a possibility,[38] as the formless, as the cause of error, failure, and distraction. For those who glorified perfection as "end," as the satisfaction of ending, the infinite as that which never comes to an end could have only a dismal nature. This, however, had to change, when instead of the end and its satisfaction, the way as such came into the focus of attention. We have already seen this shifting from end to way in the change from "perfection" to "excellence." "I am the way," says Christ, and St. Paul praises hope. It is St. Augustine who finds the metaphysical foundation for the new creed: Seeking as such is a value. St. Augustine needed a good part of his life to arrive at this truth. In his early writings—contra Academicos—he emphasizes that to know is more than to seek. But later on the balance changes, and the problem of seeking, doubting, asking, questioning is now the foundation of his whole philosophy. "Let us seek as if we find, and let us find as if we seek," is the wonderful dictum which opens a new

of "einfuehlung" and our appreciation of art was likewise an "einfuehlende" identification with the work of art.

[38] Aristotle: *Met.* XI, 10 (1066 a.) and Phys. 207 a. Proclus (*Elem. of Theol.*) reveals a change (Prop. 92).

world.[39] Augustine discovers the profundity, the depth of the soul: "Grande profundum est ipse homo,"[40] the infinity of the individual—and this infinity no longer disappears out of the mind of the great thinkers. His discovery is the source of modern philosophy: the infinite movement of seeking and questioning is certainty and truth in itself. Our seeking is not only a clue to our existence, it is existence itself.[41] Throughout the Middle Ages it is the way—and the way more than the end—which inspires philosophy, and it is the very infinity of this way which makes it sublime: the way of Dionysios, of Scotus Eriugena, the "Itinerarium" of St. Bonaventura, the spiritual and ascetic approach of Master Eckhart, and even the quiet and loving way with which Spinoza clears and widens the confused thickets that hide God.

What philosophy, however, cannot fully forget is the past and its aversion to infinity. The "bad infinity"—as Hegel calls it[42]—has its place beside the newly discovered sublime infinity, the "infinity of infinities" (Scotus Eriugena). Surely, "infinity" is "perfection,"[43] but one has to distinguish, as Bonaventura does, between the "infinitas per defectum" and the "infinitas per excessum," and the "infinitas per excessum" indeed is "summa perfectio."[44] What a long way indeed from the Greek perfection of limited completeness to the perfection of infinite excess.[45]

---

[39] Augustine: *De Trin.* IX, 1.   [40] Augustine: *Confess.* IV, 14.

[41] Augustine: *De Trin.* X, 3; X, 10, 14. *De ver. Rel.* XXXIX, 73. *Soliloqu.* II, 1.

[42] Hegel: *Logic* I C 2.

[43] Joh. Damascenus: *De Orth.* Fide 4.

[44] Bonaventura: *I Sent.* d. 35 a. I qu. 5.

[45] Duns Scotus (Op. Ox. I dist. II qu. 2 no. 27) knows an "infinitas intensiva."

Infinity in all its forms—good and bad, or at least as the good infinity—becomes a necessary and fundamental concept in all later philosophy. Albertus Magnus,[46] Thomas Aquinas,[47] even Descartes[48]—here as a strange and foreign substance in the system—use the concept of infinity, and Spinoza[49] strives again and again to grasp the full content of the new truth. The infinite exists before the finite, the finite has its existence through the infinite, the infinite is essentially indivisible—these results would have been incompatible with the Greek absolute finite perfection.

The spirit of compromise, however, is great, and in no philosopher greater than in Thomas Aquinas. He cannot forget the Aristotelian perfection, and in his ardent desire to reconcile the new truth with the old, he applies a method which proves fatal to the new idea of infinity, taking all creative power, even all meaning out of this concept. It is the method of analogy, the idea of proportion between the finite and the infinite. The astonishing paradox of an analogy between the finite and the infinite is the most extraordinary application of a method—fit for relations between rational and limited entities—to the transcendent and by no means rational sphere of infinity. In order to apply this method, Aquinas has to start from the idea of a totality of being, a complete, perfect—but infinite!—whole in which all finite things participate, some more, some less, but all in a certain proportion. It seems obvious that proportion is and can only be between finite beings, and that for the Greek—

[46] Albertus Magnus: *Summa Theol.* I, 14, 1. He knows even three kinds of infinity.

[47] Aquinas: *Summa Theol.* I, 7, 1; *Comp. Theol.* I, 7; *De Pot.* qu. 1 a. 2 c; *Gent.* I, 43.

[48] Descartes: *Med.* III and *Princ. Phil.* I, 27.

[49] Spinoza: *Ethics* I and *Letter to L. Meyer* April 20, 1663.

especially the Stoic—philosopher, whose cosmos was a finite whole, a proportion between things and cosmos was possible, as well as a proportional knowledge in regard to this cosmos. But after God had widened to an infinity and even an indivisible infinity, there was no possibility for an analogical knowledge of God. Even if Aquinas does not mean that the single finite things stand in direct proportion to God, but that the whole sphere of finite things as such stands in proportion to God, his argument does not hold: The finite things are certainly in a relation to each other, but in God there are no parts which could be in an analogical relation, as God is indivisible and infinite. Aquinas's method of analogy reduces the infinity of God to a finitude, restores the old Greek limitation and is the cause of a revival of the fallacy of divine perfection in most of the great systems of modern philosophy. It is the rationalization and mechanization of religious thought throughout the Renaissance which Aquinas's method of analogy brought into existence.[50] The dogma of Descartes' and Spinoza's attributes and their analogical correspondence, the pre-established harmony of Leibniz stand under the spell of the "infinite analogy" and glorify again complete perfection as a mechanism.[51] And this same mechanism which has entered heaven enters also the soul of men: Psychology in the fatal attempt of the associationists, Hartley, Priestley, etc., breaks the indivisible infinity of the soul into atoms and puts them together according to similarity; and from that time on for a long period men professed to know of the existence of each other by inferences of analogy.

[50] Perhaps Philo, in an attempt to compromise between Greek philosophy and the Bible, was one of the first to use analogy as an interpretation of the infinite.

[51] See Leibniz' example of the watchmaker (*Preestbl. Harmon.* 1696).

It is a healthy reaction against this transgression of analogy when Cusanus states clearly that there is not and cannot be any proportion between the finite and the infinite.[52] With this strict refusal he opens the way for the discovery of the concept of inner force and personality, the infinite "posse."[53]

III

As we passed through the Christian medieval philosophy, we saw that slowly but ever more thoroughly the old idea of perfection was changed, and this change was effected by an ever increasing significance of negation. The negation as a means of penetrating into the absolute; the negation as a conversion into utter affirmation.

In a shy and cautious way the negation turned up in Augustine's and Anselm's definition of perfection, as that than which nothing greater and better can be perceived. The perfection was here expressed negatively, and this was quite a revolutionary change. Then we saw "totality of conditions" transformed into the "unconditioned," the "totality of parts," the "whole" into the "indivisible," and at last out of the totality of limitation and completeness grew the "unlimited," the "infinity."

All this would not be astonishing at all, if negation restricted itself to negating. But these negations mentioned above are something more, they are positive, they open up a new sphere, unknown until then. And so we arrive at the central concept of this new sphere, the "NAUGHT" as such.

Bergson explains the naught as the empty place for a

---

52 Cusanus: *De Docta Ignorantia* I, 1 and 3. Instead of analogy Cusanus uses the more modest and adequate concept of "conjecture."
53 Cusanus: *De Apice Theoriae* and *De Globe Mundi.*

disappointed expectation.[54] This, however, cannot be correct, considering the pioneering role which the naught had in the philosophy of religion and in metaphysics Perhaps naught stands indeed for something—every concept stands for something, has a deeper signification, as the term itself indicates—but it surely does not stand for a disappointment. On the contrary, it stands for that which overcomes all disappointment of words, concepts, and symbols. It signifies the total conversion of evaluation in the Jewish-Christian philosophy and is then generally misunderstood, when measured by Greek standards.

The so-called negative theology and negative philosophy does not begin only with Gregory of Nyssa and Dionysios Areopagita. It begins with the first origin of religion: The unspeakable, the nameless are early attributes of the Divine. The conviction that God should not be labeled by words is a divination of a realm in which the not-speaking, not-naming has a positive signification. It is an utter misunderstanding to deduce the realm of the unknown and unnamed from our subjective mental limitation. This again would mean that we measure this new sphere according to the old standard of rational perfection, the ideal of scientific systematization. Right here we have the proof that the old ideal of perfection is the reverse of the new religious experience. The unnamable, the ineffable is absolute, unconditioned. It is not the confession of a defect but a declaration of war against a sphere which in its turn is felt as thoroughly defective.

And for this ineffable, this naught, a new attitude is wanted which does not correspond to the attitude of complete perfection, the $\theta\epsilon\omega\rho\iota\alpha$, or to mere intuition. We

[54] Bergson: *Evolution Creatrice* (7th edit.) page 301 seq.

have a divination of this attitude even in Greek thought, because it is rooted in human nature and not limited to the Jewish-Christian creed. We have it in the "$\pi\alpha\theta\epsilon\hat{\iota}\nu$" of Aristotle as distinct from the "$\mu\alpha\theta\epsilon\hat{\iota}\nu$."[55] We find it in Philo[56] and his Jewish followers: in Halevi,[57] in Maimonides.[58] And we find it in all the great Christian mystics: in Gregory of Nyssa, Augustine,[59] Dionysios, Scotus Eriugena, St. Bernard, St. Bonaventura, Eckhart, and many others. It is now a community of love with God, now a devotion and surrender—but always a dynamic approach, a fervent and ardent "excessus."

What is this mysterious power of the "naught" which rises from such deep emotional springs? This naught was there before Parmenides' being, and the Eleatic school feared in it the deadly danger of its static concept. It developed into dynamite which blasted again and again the philosophical cognition and became the driving element in the development of thought. Appeased by Plato and Aristotle into a kind of supplementary being, it does not stop being a challenge to the paradox of the total limited being, to the paradox of perfection as a complete and absolute end. It becomes the "beyond" to this perfect limitation. As long as men clung to the limited being as perfect, and closed their eyes to the paradox of this concept, the beyond, the naught seemed a danger, a chaos, a loss of all security and order. But when philosophy started to accept the challenge of the naught as a truth above the limited being—the naught became the solution of the

55 Aristotle: *Fragmenta Nr.* 15.
56 Philo: *Quis rer. div. heres sit* XIV, 68 seq. *De Post. Caini* 4, 5.
57 Halevi: *Ha Kuzari* I, 95.
58 Maimonides: *More Nebuchim* II, 36.
59 Augustine: *De ordine* 16 no. 44 and 18 no. 47.

paradox, and the beyond to the perfect limit, the absolute infinity, as naught, was adored as salvation.

It is easy to understand that the first people who had this new experience cast away the good with the bad, and that they made an hypostasis out of the naught, just as they had done before with the being. We find this exaggeration in early mysticism, in the passionate desire to abandon everything and to plunge into the immediacy of the naught. So the Divinity often assumes in Neoplatonism, in Dionysios, in Scotus, even in Eckhart, the character of absolute nothingness. This static naught, however, is not much more than the Eleatic being with a negation sign and runs through the whole Christian mystic philosophy as a Greek legacy.[60] To be sure, a negation sign means a contrast, and a contrasting naught would be a "relative naught." For this relative naught it would even be arbitrary on which side of the relation the negative pole is to be seen and on which the positive pole. The sides would be exchangeable. The only essential in all contrasts is their togetherness which is a totality, perfect and exclusive. Because of this perfection the Pythagoreans invented contrasts, wherever they were missing; for instance, the "counter-earth" $(\dot{\alpha}\nu\tau\acute{\iota}\chi\theta\omega\nu)$ as a supplement to the earth. Contrasts as thesis and antithesis form the perfect whole of a synthesis,[61] and this synthesis in all its perfection is exclusive. Therefore, logic knows

[60] The attitude towards this naught is the identifying intuition (page 38).

[61] The dialectic method of Hegel—based on thesis, antithesis, and synthesis—is therefore certainly a method of rational perfection, built on the ideal of the whole and its contrasting supplementary parts. Only in so far as Hegel gives to every achieved totality a merely transitional meaning, he surpasses the rational sphere of perfection. He, however, restitutes the ideal of perfection in claiming a final totality to which all these transitional totalities are driving.

the principle of the "excluded middle" and regards the "all" of contrasts as the foundation of all perfect and complete mental construction: The "principle of contradiction" is its basic law. This principle, however, is limited to the sphere of relativity and is usually expressed in a restricted way: A thing cannot "in the same respect" be and not be; or, a thing cannot "at the same time" be and not be.[62]

This merely "relative naught," however, cannot be the new concept of Christian philosophy. What the new philosophy discovered as the not-conditioned, not-divisible, not-finite is not the negation of contrast, but an absolute negation. The absolute itself appeared in the disguise of a negative notion, as the not-conditioned.

Can there be an absolute nothing? It can be as the negation of the whole sphere of relations, as the "nothing of relations." But this nothing of relations is not to be understood as a contrast to the sphere of relations, because if it were, it would again form a side of a relation, be an antithesis and a part of a synthesis. The absolute is not a contrast to the relative, but it overarches the field of relations as its beyond, it does not exclude this field but includes it into its wider range.

This absolute naught transcends the relation of contrast. That it preserved the name of the contrasting "naught" in early Christian thought may have its historical explanation in the fact that it was born in a spiritual struggle with the total, perfect, limited being of Greek philosophy. But its meaning is not the mere contrast to this being. It is more.

Let us take the notion of "immortality." Immortality may have developed out of the experience of death. It is,

[62] Aristotle: *Met.* 1005 b.

however, not a mere contrast with death. It includes the idea of resurrection and has been born in the minds of men together with this idea of resurrection. So immortality is not the mere opposite of death, but its overcoming; it includes the idea of death. One has to consider death in the frame of its wider scope, one has to go through death in order to arrive at immortality. Or let us take the notion of "innocence" which also exists in most languages merely in a negative form: It is not a mere opposite to "nocence," i.e. guilt; it is its overcoming. It indicates that the innocence of the child is not its highest form, but that real innocence is a quality which takes guilt into account and is able to face and overcome the temptations of the world.

So language indicates in some of its most important concepts that there is a negation which has an embracing quality, constituting a realm where the one includes, not excludes, the other. The meaning of this "absolute negation" is, therefore, in every respect different from that of contrast. While in contrast, in the total limited sphere the one and the other deprive each other, are their mutual privation[63]—here the other is that which enriches the one, carries it to a height. It is the infinite, the infi-

[63] It may have been this insight in the narrow and envious atmosphere of the limited total system, where the "other" always is the enemy of the "one" that Cusanus tried in his work: "De non aliud" to formulate God's essence as the "not-other." There is an endeavor of infinite understanding in this concept which overcomes all theories of contrast, as they generally turn up in consequence of mental dissections and constructions. Another, but desperate, attempt of Cusanus to overcome the contrasting dissection, was his "coincidentia oppositorum" with which already Heraclitus had tried to conquer the pessimism of contrasts. But the relation of identity seems unsuitable as a solution to the problem. It remains just a paradox and shows, as paradoxes do, only the desperation of the human mind.

nite possibility as an inexhaustible resource which is at the core of this naught; possibility, not in contrast to actuality—as it was in Greek philosophy—but possibility as excelling and exceeding the actual. Δύναμις for the first time in history is more, not less, than the actual.

This beyond to all limitation and relation is what Scotus Eriugena meant when he called the naught "excellentia,"[64] and what Bernard and Bonaventura meant when they called the infinite "excess." The Christian philosophy, however, found another concept which was used increasingly in the new era, but not always realized in all its implications. This was the SIMPLE. The simple in Greek philosophy and in the Renaissance is a part in relation to the compound, a last part. But the simple which now is an expression of transcendence, of the absolute, is not a part, not a "one." It signifies the individual, but surpasses the notion of mere uniqueness and indivisibility which are of the essence of individuality. The simple is an indivisible which not only transcends all division, but in its transcending keeps the divisibility as overcome in the frame of its concept. We have this phenomenon whenever we incorrectly say that something is not divisible into its parts without a "remainder," or that the whole is more than the sum of its parts.[65] I say "incorrectly," because a whole which leaves a remainder besides its parts and which is more than its parts, is for that reason no whole. It excels and exceeds the category

[64] Scotus Eriugena: *De Divis. Nat.* III, 14. Dionysios (*De Div. Nom.* IV, 3 and VII, 2) uses "excessus."

[65] Proclus (*Elem. of Theol.* Prop. 67) seems to see a similar truth, when he distinguishes between the "whole-before-the-parts" and the "whole-of-parts." But he falls back on the Platonic idea of "wholeness" (εἶδος ὁλότητος; Prop. 69).

of the whole. The simple is, as distinguished from the one, a negation.[66] [67] It negates the manifoldness, but in negating this manifoldness, it is its transcendence. The discovery of the simple by overcoming something composed and complicated produces a surprise; when we have tried hard to understand something, we are surprised suddenly to find it very simple. With the simple we mean also the manifold, not as excluded but as included, and we therefore consider the simple together with its unfolding. A simple is never only a whole; we can consider it as if it be a mere whole of the unfolded, of the manifold. But if we do this, we abstract from the beyond which makes it the simple. There are, therefore, two ways of looking at the world: one inadequate which sees only the parts, the manifold and its togetherness in a whole;[68] and one adequate which sees this whole of parts, but transcended, overcome by a beyond which transforms it into simplicity.

The simple is a new and essential concept of metaphysics, an important attribute of God, like the infinite. It replaces the old idea of perfection. It does so even in the system of Descartes, although it is there merely adopted in the old meaning of a contrast to the compound or as "last part." It is Kant who, after having discussed the

---

[66] See Aristotle's distinction between ἁπλοῦς = simple and ἒν = one, *Met.* 1072 a.

[67] Kant states the absolute and the negative character of the "simple": "Ein Object sich als einfach vorstellen, ist ein bloss *negativer* Begriff, der der Vernunft unvermeidlich ist, weil er allein das *Unbedingte* zu allem Zusammengesetzten enthaelt." (Uber eine Entdeckung, nach der alle neue Critik etc. 1 c.)

[68] Another and the opposite inadequacy may be found in Bergson's "élan vital." With his "élan" and "durée" as an indistinguishable stream he considers only the beyond, eliminating the manifold without which there cannot be any beyond. Therefore his "durée" is an abstraction and he has difficulty in placing the manifold back in the world.

pitfalls of an uncritical metaphysics, finds the truth in his "regulative idea" of God as the "simple," as the ground which lives beyond all "aggregate," all mere summing up and totality.[69] Here is an inkling that "totality" can only be conceived in the beyond of a simplicity, and that our so-called urge *for* totality is in reality an urge which transcends totality and because of this transcendence is able to limit and constitute totalities in this world.

The simple now also becomes a basic concept for the knowledge of the soul, for psychology and ethics. Simplicity is a Christian virtue, as an expression of personality. Here simplicity means maturity as a concentration of our experiences. Maturity is always simple. Even in the field of science simplicity is a concentration; the scientific "simplifications," when not merely artificial constructions of a symbolizing intellect,[70] may be called "abstractions,"[71] but nevertheless are shaped by a concentrating power.

The "simple" which we tried to deduce here—although it is difficult to mold it into a concept—is what we call "FORCE." Force is always simple because it is the beyond of its unfolding. Force is manifestation, but it is also beyond manifestation. It is always immanent, a latent force; but it is also always transcendent as an operating force. It appears as a drive toward a being and at the same time an overcoming of this being. It is a movement of intention and at the same time a challenge to the intended. Force is not cause, even not "first cause," at Plato put it in his *Phaedrus* with regard to the soul and in his *Laws* with regard to God.[72] A "first cause" is only a thing and it

---

69 Kant: *Critique of Pure Reason*, 2nd ed. page 607.

70 See page 71.

71 On "abstraction" see Kant: *Versuch den Begriff der negativ.* Groessen etc. III.   72 Plato: *Phaedrus* 245; *Laws* 896.

stands first in a row of causes, united with other causes into a totality, into a completeness and perfection of causes. A "first cause" is always the "last end" of thinking, it is always also "last end,"[73] and in this circle of "final cause" the cosmos rounds out into a perfect whole.[74]

No, to break out of the line of cause and effect is the task of the new metaphysics and it does so in discovering the concept of force which is not a first and not a last, but is always unique, simple, and infinite, and therefore outside of the line. To proceed from mere causation to force means an overcoming. In this overcoming negation changes into affirmation, and this discovery was made not only by Leibniz, when he found his new concept of force[75] and personality—foreshadowed in the thoughts of Augustine and Cusanus—but also by Kant, when he based his philosophy on the concept of freedom, converted from the mere negative, empirical freedom into the positive, "intelligible," and infinite freedom. Kant here is at once a revolutionary and continues the great tradition of medieval philosophy.

This reverse of force from negation to affirmation surpasses the framework of our intellectual constructions and has, whenever our mind gets to work on it, to be remodeled into a relation of contrasts. So the manifoldness which force transforms into simplicity is understood intellectually as a negation and contrast to force. We speak of "resistance" to force, of matter as "resisting" force. Our thinking is always at work constructing a duality of pendants, in order to bring them together in a

[73] Duns Scotus: *De Prim.* Princ. 3.

[74] Aquinas is right from his point of view in basing divine perfection also on the concept of "first cause" (*Summa Theol.* I qu. 4 a. 2).

[75] Leibniz: *De Prim. Phil. Emend. et de Notione Subst.*

relational unity, as a symbol of the whole and the parts. And so force and matter build a whole in which the one lives at the expense of the other. Or matter is even more apparently conceived as a contrast by considering it as a resisting, negating counter force. This duality of contrasting, polar forces—one turned against the other and one like the other—results in zero, as $+2$ and -2 make zero. Zero as the outcome of this intellectual interpretation appears here as a symbol of the all.[76]

Not contrast, however, not resistance, characterizes the realm of force. Force is above contrast, force lives not only at the expense of its so-called resistance, but also concentrates and enhances it as its own manifestation. And so advancing more and more into a realm which will never be satisfactorily cleared by rational thinking, we arrive at last at the problem of creation, inseparable from the idea of force and personality.

CREATION could not come into the focus of research before men had discovered the togetherness of the simple and the manifold, of force and resistance, of the infinite and the finite. Where there was merely limitation, as in Greek thought, merely satisfaction and perfection, a world-order could rise, but never a world-creation.[77] World-order means insight in the law of parts and their whole, and a clear knowledge of the ordered whole. God was then the order of the world, at best the philosopher, whose mind ever clearer, more distinct, and more complete arranges the relations in the ready substance.

Creation, however, is more. Here is not a total substance, ready to be ordered; here is first of all: nothing.

[76] So in Schelling's Metaphysics of Indifference; see page 24.

[77] Empedocles calls creation, genesis ($\phi\acute{\upsilon}\sigma\iota\varsigma$) a mere word. According to him there is nothing but mixture and separation. (Diels: loc. cit. 226 Frag. 8.)

Without this nothing no created being can come to birth. It is therefore no accident—and surely no embarrassment —that creation begins for all of its great prophets, for Origines, Dionysios, Scotus, Maimonides, Eckhart, Cusanus, etc., as a creation out of nothing: creatio ex nihilo. Just because the "created" is perceived as a whole, as an all, as a complete world, it can only appear with its counterpart, the naught. It is this naught out of which the all not only bursts, but which also links and ties it together. The naught is not only the source but also the beyond of the "created" and leads the created finite into infinity. The naught which Scotus calls "excellentia" and the infinite which Bonaventura calls "excessus" are excellent and exceeding with regard to the finite totality of the created world. Creation is for these philosophers the transition of naught over being to naught—sometimes falsely conceived as a return. It is the infinite process of an infinite creative force which now assumes the attribute of perfection, because it excels and exceeds the "imperfect" world of created things. Imperceptibly force, as potentiality, assumes the character of perfection. God is the "infinite posse"[78] which is a surplus beyond all merely actual being.

Here, however, we are in danger again of conceiving the naught as a contrast to being and to confront the creative force with a resisting matter. It is from time immemorial a requisite of an intellectual cosmology to show God in a fierce fight with chaotic matter. Yet: if the creative force is in contrast with matter, then creation becomes destruction, and this interpretation does not agree with the fact that God himself creates this hostile matter also. Nevertheless, it may be allowed—and always

[78] Cusanus: *De Ludo Globi* I. De Apice Theoriae.

will be—to explain creation partly as a destruction. One must, however, be aware that this is only a metaphorical saying and that every so-called destruction is at the same time a rise and new birth. So there is nothing purely negative in the world—"but thinking makes it so."

Thinking in relations cannot get at the core of creation and in so far—but only in so far—Aristotle and Aquinas were right to deny a "relation" between God and the world. Wrong, however, was Aristotle in cutting God entirely off from the world, not because relation as such seemed inadequate, but because he saw God only in a relation of identity with himself. And wrong was Aquinas in comparing God with a lifeless column, indifferent to the relations which creatures may have to it.[79] It is not lifelessness which makes the relation here impossible. On the contrary, because God is life, the merely static rational relation does not suffice. The living force of divine creation refuses the separation which every intellectual relation necessarily requires.

Nor do "possible" and "actual" stand in a relation of contrast and exclusion to each other, as there cannot be any creation when the possible is excluded from God in the way of Thomism and Aristotelian philosophy. In force and creation the possible and the actual are united in potentiality.[80] The possible has a wider range than the actual, the actual being in the light of creation always a possible in the flux and process of becoming.

The static world-view of ancient thought comes into movement. Time becomes the most burning problem. It is a finite present bursting out of the infinite nonexistent

[79] Aquinas: *Summa Theol.* I qu. 13 a. 7.

[80] Leibniz says with regard to force: "Vis activa inter facultatem agendi actionemque ipsam media est et conatum involvit atque ita per se ipsam in operationem fertur." (*De prim. phil. Emend. et de Not. Substant.*)

past and flowing into an equally infinite and nonexistent beyond, the future. Seen, however, from the present, which is a moment in the flow from past to future, time divides backwards into the past and forward into the future, and past and future, abstracted from the beyond, are constructed as parts of a whole, similar to the finite present, forming with the present a whole of parts, a row of past, present, and future. Here again we experience the double way of reflection: As the realization of force could be considered not only in the movement to its beyond, but also abstracted from the beyond as an unfolded whole and divisible objectivation,[81] so creation can be observed in a double way: inadequately and eliminating the beyond we may regard it as a whole of parts, as an adaptation of the infinite past and future to the finite present. Here past and future become, in memory and expectation, finite presents too: the present of past and the present of future,[82] forming an enlarged present of phases which we call our earthly time, divisible and objective. For this limited "all," for this manifold and total quantity the famous problems of Scholastic philosophy indeed are valid: Has this world a beginning, has it an end, in space and time?

If we, however, consider creation really as creation, as simple and as beyond to all unfolding, then creation "sub specie aeternitatis" transcends itself as a present which is a transition from eternity to eternity. And then space and time become the simple, indivisible potentiality which beyond all created things represents the uniqueness and infinity of creation.

The problem of creation is indeed scarcely moldable into conceptual knowledge and it lives, therefore, only in

[81] See page 50.
[82] Augustine: *Conf.* XI, 26.

the paradoxical truths of the great thinkers. Is Eckhart's God the nothing, is he being? What does his "nu," the moment, mean in relation to eternity? What his "work" in relation to the "detachment of all work?" It is the problematic unfolding of the limit in the unlimited, the "nu" in eternity, an unfolding which is also a return to simplicity, a negation and refusal. It is the will who needs the work, but also is beyond all works, a doing which is an undoing too, a forming which is also a criticizing, judging, and condemning of that which is formed. And this seemingly contrasting movement is essential too for the creation of knowledge, of inquiry which limits itself in answers, but again and again transforms these answers into questions. It challenges the answer, raises in every answer the naught of Socratic ignorance, "ignorantia docta," and so—wandering from question to question in the problematic depth of the mind—grows into the beyond of all answers and guarantees the infinite process of seeking and inquiry.

3

HUMANITY AND DIVINE

PERFECTION

I

BECAUSE of the deeply felt relation between God and world the problem of divine perfection is not reserved for heaven alone, but is found also as a divine reflection shining upon this world and residing in the creative and in the ethical power of men. We have, therefore, to go into the problem of perfection also in regard to aesthetics and ethics.

Is the idea of perfection justified in art?—this is our first concern.

It was the problem of creation which we broached as the last problem in the realm of the divine, and it should be the problem of creation again which is at the heart of aesthetics, at least since Christian philosophy has dared to approach this problem at all. In fact, however, the Greek inheritance is in this field also so great that the way seems completely barred to this central and fundamental problem of art. Not creation but order was for many centuries the important aesthetic problem, form in relation to matter, and we should not in the least be surprised to find as standard and ideal of aesthetic order the old idea of perfection. In the field of art, of poetry indeed, people say, perfection has its very own sphere. We find so little or no perfection in life, so little or no satisfaction, that art, the beautiful appearance and fiction, may and shall feign that which life denies us, and we dream in art to achieve and to hold that which the Divine really is: perfection.

If we investigate this belief first by simple common sense, we see that a "perfect artist" is about as impossible as a "perfect God." Is there a "perfect genius," a "complete genius"? Or does it not contradict the idea of a genius, to be complete and perfect? And indeed we see that here as everywhere we use perfection only in a limited and inferior sphere. We can speak of a "perfect technician," of a "perfect mastering of color," of "perfect treatment of the brush," of a "perfect resemblance of portrait to model." All that, however, does not make the work of art. On the contrary, a masterpiece is found only where all these perfections are somehow overcome, where we are not aware of them. It is always the sign of a failure in art when we are aware first and mostly of those things which can be perfect; in other words, when we are inclined to concentrate on the mere technique,[1] the likeness, the purpose of the artist, etc. It is this that we call "routine." A "perfect artist" would be a "perfect routinier," a virtuoso. To be sure, there are plenty of people who adore virtuosity and nothing but it—these people, however, are not the ones who penetrate deeply into the essence of art. For them there is no great difference between the virtuoso and an ape climbing a tree with dexterity. The real lover of art will, on the contrary, be repelled or remain unmoved, cold, and indifferent toward the work of mere virtuosity.

Who would call Dante's *Divina Comedia* a perfect work? But there could be a "perfect commentary" to Dante's masterwork, a commentary which in an exhaus-

[1] The modern hypostasis of technique as such, technique as highest achievement and meaning of the world, is another consequence of the old ideal of perfection.

tive, distinct, and clear way treats all questions belonging in the limited field of a commentary.

It was the great deed of Kant to eliminate the concept of perfection from aesthetics, a contribution which has not been given the recognition which it deserves. This Kantian progress made aesthetics possible for the first time. And with his sagacity Kant saw that the wrong aesthetic concept of perfection was rooted in the idea of end, of purpose. So he challenged the idea of "end" in art and emphasized that pure beauty is to be found only where a work does not reveal an end, an interest. The rule of the end was here seriously attacked, even in a field where it seemed unassailable—in the field of human action. The "beautiful," Kant states, has nothing to do with any conceptual entity, therefore is not concerned with the concept of purpose and the conformity to purpose which is perfection.[2] But Kant went still further: He not only discovered the beautiful as indifferent to end and perfection, but also in the second aesthetic entity, the SUBLIME, he discovered a sphere which is a repulsion, a destruction and violation of end and perfection, a total negation of these values.[3] Here is the culminating point of this new aesthetics: That which is inexpedient, inadequate, a negation to end and purpose, that which in the highest degree is imperfect (in the old sense), the challenge to perfection and satisfaction is aesthetically sublime.[4]

[2] Kant: *Critique of Judgment* § 15, 16.

[3] Kant: *Critique of Judgment* § 23.

[4] It would be unfair not to mention a work which is full of fine observations and certainly has influenced Kant: E. Burke's *Inquiry into the Origin of the Sublime and Beautiful*. Burke too sees that perfection and end are unessential for beauty and that the sublime is a notion of highest importance. He, however, is unable to find the fundamental princi-

Had Kant transferred these ideas to the realm of religious philosophy, the findings of R. Otto, his divine "mysterium tremendum" would have been anticipated. Here indeed was the mysterium tremendum, and it was here in the aesthetic concept of the "sublime" as that which is sublime, because it triumphs over any purpose.

Although admirable and audacious in destruction, in criticism, in clearing away the misinterpretations of the past, Kant was cautious in constructing, and so he fell back on the prejudices of the eighteenth century, on the world of ends. This he did in inventing the concept of "subjective purposiveness." He originated this hybrid concept in order to keep the beautiful from sliding entirely out of the realm of ends, in order to compromise with the Greek world of perfection, balance, and complete totality. Men could not yet do without ends; what had no end was not serious; only the rational end had meaning in the eyes of a people possessed by the holiness of finality. Even Schiller interpreted Kant's aesthetics in a dangerous way, in shifting art—detached from ends—into the sphere of games, and so created the fatal play-theory of art, the most fatal of all art theories, which satisfied the public for a long time. This theory more than anything else made it impossible to apply the new truth of "creation without end" to the religious sphere and to deepen the problem of divine creation. God's creation of the world would have been in danger of turning into a mere game.

Kant's return to the final sphere was—as far as art was concerned—comparatively harmless. Here his conviction

ple. The beautiful is mere relaxation and the sublime is horror which works our senses up, makes us labour and thus serves self-preservation—a kind of sensuous massage.

that art has nothing to do with ends and perfection was so deeply rooted that his compromise with the past merely caused a new formation of words: "subjective purposiveness without purpose," a phrase which contradicts itself.[5] And, in fact, Kant's subjective purposiveness has nothing in common with ends, but results merely out of his dissection of the mind into separate capacities, the unification of which he represents under the term of "subjective purposiveness."

The real return to the realm of ends was done in the "teleological judgment," the second part of the *Critique*, which, more than any other Kantian work, glorifies the end and even attempts to state an ultimate end of world-creation. Here, indeed, the ideal of ancient perfection is brought to its climax, and the ingenious new truth which had been gained for the human artist was abandoned in regard to the divine Creator. To achieve this result, Kant bases his theory of a natural internal purposiveness on the living organism. Here in the living organism not only do the parts form the whole as its means, but they also serve each other as means and ends, causes and effects, and stand in a relation of reciprocity. This Kantian argument certainly has some truth, but it is not the whole truth; it is an abstraction, one-sided and born of the desire to surrender to finality. It is quite obvious that in the living organism parts not only mutually build, but also destroy, each other, wear out and consume each other. This is the nature of life that it not only grows but also fades, not only lives through itself but also lives at the expense of itself. The fact of death—although deeply rooted in life—is undoubtedly a

[5] Kant: *Critique of Judgment* § 11.

highly inexpedient phenomenon. Not the "organism" therefore, but at best the "organization" could serve as an example for an objective finality, and Kant indeed mentions this example.[6] The organization is in fact a balance and totality of means and ends, and it has the advantage of not dying, at least not of a natural death. This advantage, however, does not make it a suitable example for natural finality, because—in contrast to the organism—it is not nature, but mental construction. Just because it is this and only this, can it serve as an example for finality which always is constructed, arbitrary, and abstract. Only the creation of a world which would be a constructed organization, not a living world, could have an "ultimate end." This organized world would be a correct example for the ideal of perfection, and its Creator would be an intelligent, methodical, calculating mind, it would be God as the director of a well functioning organization. Therefore, there is in reality not a very great difference between this Kantian idea of world-finality and the Spinozist ideal of an organized world-substance. Also, Spinoza's world-substance, its analogies, hierarchies, its system of modes tend to an ever increasing clarity of a Cartesian mechanism, and God is here perfection and ultimate goal, totality and completeness, to which all modes are striving.

II

What Kant discovered in his concept of the sublime was the fact that the depth of art is a beyond to the world of ends and perfection, a refusal even of this world, in favor of a higher world. Had he followed this

[6] Kant: *Critique of Judgment* § 65.

idea, he would have found the TRAGIC as the soul of all art. Because the tragic is the failure of our ends, this failure is so much greater and more moving the wider the radius of ends is drawn and the more perfect and secure the planning seems, rooted in the person of the hero. And this hero is a hero because the greatness and perfection of his final world breaks down; his greatness as man manifests itself in the beyond which for him is death, and for the spectator resurrection.

Therefore, not merely death, an ending and cessation, is the meaning of tragedy, but rather the beyond of resurrection, of uplifting. All theories of tragedy prove erroneous which are based on pessimism, on a quietistic ideal of nirvana, on an eternal rest of the will—as if the will were identical with its ends and were buried in the ruins of its ends. On the contrary, tragedy teaches that the will lives in the triumph over ends, and that it rises out of their collapse to its infinity. Tragedies do not end with the fifth act, the tension of the five acts is only an opening to their beyond; the tragedy does not occupy a space of time—as mere entertainment does—but transforms time into the naught, out of which creation rises and which signifies eternity.

And as in the art of tragedy and poetry, so it is in all other spheres of art; in painting, sculpture, etc. What the painter needs and cannot do without is the world of things in their manifoldness, independence, and purposive form, "nature" in all its riches. But he needs this manifoldness only to overcome it, to submerge it in a beyond, in space, light, atmosphere, color, and shadow. Subject matter is this manifoldness of things which is overcome in the work of art. There is no great art without subject matter—the so-called "abstract" painting and sculpture is a misunderstanding or exaggeration of a right principle, just as is the striving of the mystic to grasp God without images and to plunge into the empty nothingness of the divine.[7] There can be no great art, however, without the overcoming of subject matter, without the concentration, simplification, and enhancement of "nature," a concentration which may even result in a distortion of the "natural" form and independent meaning of things. It is this overcoming, concentration, and simplification which we call "STYLIZATION." And we call "IMITATION" the mere surrender to the purposive, expedient, natural manifoldness of things. Imitation alone never makes a work of art. In times, when the expedient perfection, the technical skill seemed the core of art, imitation was everything and the perfect imitation, i.e. "illusion," was the goal of painting. So a Greek painter, Zeuxis, could earn praise for painting cherries so "natural" that birds picked at them. The Greek aesthetics therefore, based on skill and perfection, never advanced much beyond the principle of mere imitation—μίμησις was here the meaning of art.[8] Imitation, however, is nothing but the pursuit of a goal set up before the artist, just as all purposive action is a kind of imitation, a repetition of that which the end meant. Imitation, illusion does not penetrate into the core of art. The problem of illusion, of artistic appearance, has been rather overrated. The problem of artistic reality behind and above this appearance is a more vital problem, and

[7] Landscape painting may come near to the ideal of abstract painting, developing into an expression of the infinity of atmosphere, light, sky, clouds; and so it indeed developed in a somehow parallel line with the "abstract music," changing from a mere accompaniment or background to the main subject of art.

[8] Plato: *Repub*. 596 seq. But compare *Symp*. 211. Aristotle: *Pol*. VIII, 5. But compare *Poet*. II and IX, where a certain idealization as a beyond to imitation is recommended. In this line Plotinus: *Ennead*. V, 8, 1.

although it is to be found in all religious cosmologies, attached to the problem of divine creation, searching for a reality behind the "veil of the Maya," it has been largely neglected in the aesthetic systems. To stop at the sphere of imitation and appearance, however, means to stop at the immature level of the student. It is the scholarly part in the life of the artist which is devoted to imitation, to the study of "nature," to copying in a perfect way. Perfect imitation, perfection is the preparatory school of art. The laws of our school-aesthetics, the rules of perspective, of complementary coloring, of the deception of the senses are preparatory schooling. The student has to learn them, but the master has to go beyond.

The student has to learn them because it is the paradox of all art that the work of art is as well "made" as "created."[9] So far as it is made, it belongs to the sphere of divisibility, is a whole, has parts, is final and perfect, can be criticized, has defects, and can be an object of rational aesthetics. So far as it is a living creation, however—and only in so far is it art—it transcends the categories of part, whole, and composition and is plainly simple. It is the queer aspect of human art that creation is possible only in the way of making. The work grows into its beyond, into life and infinity only by limitation, reflection, criticism; only by that which is purposed and perfected can the infinite creation be raised. The artificial, expedient, final building of the manifold, called "composition," all this work matured in knowledge and technical skill, however, would in all its perfection leave us indifferent as mere routine were there not the beyond, the transgression beyond the closed thing. This beyond carries us away the more the arrangement of architec-

[9] It is this the double aspect which we considered, discussing the simplicity of force and creation. (Pages 50 and 56.)

tonic composition, of proportion, and balance seems self-sufficient. It is this which terrifies all young artists: all the teachable laws of composition, exist only in order to be sacrificed to a beyond which can neither be taught nor learned, because it is never really "known": the style. The artist himself and his time are scarcely ever aware of "style." The artist creates it, his time misunderstands it. What the time alone understands and discusses are the rules of the schools. It is left to the coming generations to decide whether a time had only schools and their fight for the authority of their rules, or whether there was a style, to which unwillingly and unknowingly the schools submitted.

The real problem of art, therefore, the problem of style, begins beyond the perfect making, the knowledge of rules, their imitation, critique, and aesthetic approval. Style, stylization is beyond imitation. Greek aesthetics would not have stopped at the youthful stage of imitation had it learned a lesson from Egyptian sculpture. Egyptian statues show the finest skill of imitation, extraordinary realism, and respect for "nature." But all this realism is overcome by a violent and sublime stylization, a simplification and concentration which means a spiritual transcendence, a beyond. It was the doctrine of immortality, grown out of the Osiris cult, which gave birth to the great Egyptian art as a service to resurrection and immortality.

It seems, however, as if there is one element in art which contradicts strongly the drive beyond: the frame. The frame is a definite limitation and emphasizes the walling up, the closing and finishing of the work, its total perfection and exclusiveness. And indeed, the frame has helped to propagate the erroneous idea that the closed, framed, limited thing which we hang on our walls is a perfection, and that perfection is the aim and meaning of art. Greece, too, has its share in the acknowledgment of this idea. In Greek sculpture, indeed, the frame seems to close and finish and exclude. The frame exists even before the statues or reliefs fill it, as we see it in the gable-statues and metope-reliefs of the Greek temples. In Christian art, however, in Romanesque and Gothic sculpture and painting, the frame loses this character of a fence around a perfect and self-sufficient thing; it assumes —wherever we find it as an architectural frame around the statue or as a wooden frame around the painting—a concentrating force, and in concentrating it helps to mold the parts into a simplicity of force which presses against the frame and seems to burst and transcend its limits.[10]

The closed, finished character of the work of art, its exclusiveness, therefore, exists merely for a superficial observer. The slogan: "art for art's sake" is based on this superficial attitude toward art as perfection and toward the work of art as an exclusive totality and complete-

[10] It would lead away from the main purpose of this work, if we went too far into the problems of aesthetics with regard to the various arts. So we touch only lightly the problems of music. Here the beyond, the dynamic character is so deeply rooted in the very beginnings of the great western music that we even have difficulty in segregating a field of limited and static perfection. Already the division into 12 chromatic tones and their combination is ruled by the principle of tension and results in a certain impure dissonance—impure and dissonant when compared with the purity and perfection of the overtones and the octave. And the astonishing development of the western music is a development away from the emptiness of the perfect octave to an ever increasing tension, increasing conquest of the field of dissonances, to the polyphony which was possible only because of the genuine "impurity" and tension of our tone-system. It is not accidental that the Greeks did not find their way to a polyphonic music and that Plato (*Laws* 700 seq. and 799 seq.) warned against the danger of a music of tension which stood for infinity and against perfection.

ness. But just as wrong is the slogan "art for use" which turns the work of art into a means for the needs of human life. Surely, works of art can be used for entertainment, decoration, instruction. All that usefulness, however, is not essential, just as men do not love because love is useful, or have religion because religion is expedient. The slogans "art for art's sake" and "art for use" are both offspring of the same wrong and dangerous theory of "purposive perfection," and their difference results merely from the more or less arbitrary way, how to limit the purpose. We will find the same phenomenon in ethics, where the followers of "self-perfection" fight a brother-fight against the followers of "utilitarianism."[11] There is no purpose in the work of art nor is this work of art a means for a purpose outside of its range. There is a beyond, however, and the work serves this beyond. But service is not usefulness. We will see the difference when we come to the sphere of ethics.[12]

This service of art, the transcendence of the modest object beyond its limits, is what we call EXPRESSION. In "expression," the manifoldness and perfect independence of the things disappear in a simplicity which is simple because it overcomes this manifoldness. Expression is an overcoming and can be understood as a kind of negation: expression of death is a breaking of its power and a divination of immortality; expression of suffering is its conquest and a transition to joy. Negation, however, also

[11] Page 77.

[12] Page 88. The character of service is also well manifested by the worthlessness of the material of the great works of art: paper, wood, linen, lifeless stone. We resent it therefore as decadent when precious material is used in fine art: jewels, gold, etc. And we should resent it also when collectors' vanity forces pretentious frames on pictures or builds pompous museum-palaces, putting emphasis on that which serves and thereby distracts from the essential.

here does not mean contrast. There is no "contrast" in the realm of creation, because contrast is a purely intellectual pattern. Therefore there is no ugliness as a contrast to beauty in art. The ugly, that which is in its parts and their mere togetherness disharmonious, may be pure beauty in its beyond. We call this ugliness expressive. Ugliness as expressive is beautiful. It is not to be wondered at that times which discovered the inner force of personality conquered also—in the realm of art—the so-called ugliness as expressiveness. So did the Egyptians, the Hellenistic Greeks under oriental influence, and in the highest degree Christian art in the Romanesque, Gothic, and Baroque period, where the deeply moving Passion, the torture and death of Christ, was the main subject of expression. On the other hand, the so-called pure beauty and balance of harmony has always been in danger of turning into a boring emptiness. We call it, rightly, void of expression. This inexpressive beauty was the ideal of a superficial and playful art, as that of some Greek statues of the fourth century or some representations of human life in Renaissance and Rococo. Beauty and ugliness, regularity and irregularity, harmony and disharmony—these contrasts may play a certain role in the field of workmanship although they are here often arbitrarily used and exchangeable, as the positive and negative pole. In the living work of art, however, they lose their meaning of contrast and the one seems to overgrow and develop into the other.

Expression is an awkward and indistinct term and merely substitutes something inexpressible. It is that which language has in common with art. The words of language are "expressions," at least in young languages. As Heraclitus states, language veils as well as reveals. It veils, when one takes the limited word as such; it reveals, when one realizes its beyond. Every expression of language is a closed kernel which attempts to break open. Therefore young languages are metaphorical, the metaphor being an attempt to break limits and to widen the expression until it makes divine something unexpressed. In the song, in lyric poetry, language is still involved in this movement beyond, in which the word, the phrase, lead to something unexpressed, unintended, which we call mood or atmosphere. Languages which grow old change to mere routine, to technique of expediency, especially scientific languages, where expressions are more and more restricted to plain symbols.

It is a characteristic feature of our time that the problem of expression has been pushed aside and replaced by the entirely different "symbol." In our world grown old, the attempt is made to explain every expression in language and even in art as a "symbol." The symbol is a final abstraction, a rational simplification of something more differentiated; it is a means for perfect usefulness. Symbol is always a means and always a means for an end, its so-called signification, which obviously is limited as all ends are. As a symbol, a limited entity stands for another limited entity,[13] and it is just this which makes the symbol accidental, conventional, and arbitrary. There are always different possibilities to symbolize according to the end which is intended, be it a didactic, a propagandistic end, or any other reason of simplification. The symbol, therefore, serves as general rational explanation in times when men are absorbed by nothing but their ends. So the Sophists meant to discover

[13] Leibniz therefore calls the "symbolic" or "blind" knowledge an abbreviation for an object, the explanation of which could also, if needed, be given unabbreviated. (*Medit. de cognitione, veritate et ideis.*)

the symbolic and purely conventional nature of language, and the pragmatistic and sensualistic attempts of modern symbolism are in the same line. Professional, scientific languages—as the language of mathematics—were made models for a symbolic perfection. In art it is at best the advertising poster which is a symbolic, propagandistic simplification for a purpose. Wherever art turns out to serve propaganda, it indeed becomes symbolical, but only there; and there it may be "perfect" propaganda.

Symbols belong to the category of parts and whole, expression never. Symbols simplify in substituting a part for a more complicated whole, make the part a whole and let this whole stand for the other whole which is meant. A symbol—as a means for an end called "signification"—has always its emphasis outside of itself in this its signification. Every symbol has therefore to be explained; it needs this explanation, without which it is nothing. The artistic expression, on the contrary, does not need any explanation, there is no explanation outside of it; it has to be understood by itself. The symbol is always in a relation to its signification, and this may be a relation of proportion, a relation of similarity. It may be close to analogy which acts in the same way as a means for perfection and completeness.[14] Its principle is: "pars pro toto," a principle which has been applied very wrongly to the primitive sphere of early expression. The primitive tribes, however, think so little in the category of parts and whole that they take things which *we* see as parts, not at all as parts, nor do they relate them to a whole, but believe them to be an immediate expression of something infinite, a force. The nail, the hair of a man does not stand here as a part of the body, but are expressions of a

[14] See page 41.

force of the soul, and by it the savage believes he has immediate possession of the infinite soul itself. "Body" as whole is so unimportant to him that his faith in metempsychosis makes the body a mere transition. In the same way we—wherever we feel human life—take body also as a transition to the soul, and so come in understanding and love into an immediate relation with something which is beyond the body and for which the body is only an "expression." The body as a whole, as the whole man, as pars pro toto, as symbol for another whole comes into appearance only when it stands for the whole of "species man," or for the whole of society. In the scientific and social sphere indeed the human symbol is valid as "persona," as a bodily whole which in its space-time limitation serves as a certain means in regard to the greater whole of species and society, fulfilling its final role. Symbol and finality belong together, as finality and perfection. Here in the field of science and society man is a body which by propagation is a means to species and by his social role and profession is in symbolic reference to society, signifies something for society. It is expediency and usefulness which make the symbol "man" a part and a means for the whole of "species man" and society.

Quite different, however, is "man" in the realm of expression. Man as an individual, as a personality, is no symbol and in no relation of expediency. He is an expression of that which we call "humanity," and humanity is the infinity for which no symbol exists, because it does not stand in the category of ends.[15] Humanity is not a group, not a totality, it has no parts and is no whole, it is in no way limited and in no way perfect. It is no genus and no species. But it lives in every man and every man

[15] See page 91 and 94.

feels with the best he is that he expresses humanity. Every portrait of Rembrandt presents the individual in this, his infinite beyond. Therefore his men and women show a humbleness, as if they are under a power greater than they; they are an image of frailty which may be tragic, but in the way in which tragedy is uplifting because it links us to the infinite beyond.

The truth which art manifests, and the knowledge which expression reveals is: the individual is an expression of the infinite. And so art touches the realm of religion. It is interesting indeed to see how, even in the realm of religion, symbolism tried to conquer the field and smooth down the great problems which a lively and expressive religiousness had laid before mankind. It needed the vigorous fight of Athanasius and the powerful decision of the Council of Nicaea, to overcome the wrong dogma of symbolism, of mere similarity and analogy which Arianism had taught in regard to the individual and its relation to God."[16] The individual was restored as an immediate expression of divine infinity, it was not only similar to this infinity, not only a symbol, it was more: the individual was holy, and Christ through his martyrdom had conquered the holiness of the individual, its divine nature for all eternity.

Not only in art and religion, but also in the realm of metaphysics, the conflict between symbol and expression goes on. The ideal of perfection, which is the ideal of rational knowledge, drives toward symbolism and every science calls itself "exact," when it succeeds in arranging its concepts into a closed system of clear and distinct symbols, of simplified signs. All answers of science are symbols and stand in the completeness of an unchange-

16 In this dogmatic dispute the term "ὁμοιούσιος" stands for symbolical and the term "ὁμοούσιος" for expressive.

able, static, and limited whole which is absolute and perfect. Metaphysics, however, makes the question emerge out of all answers and draws the static perfect answer into the infinite movement of inquiry.[17] Metaphysics sees the problem everywhere—let us know as seekers, says St. Augustine—here answers are no wholes, no parts, but only expressions of the infinite movement of questioning, of challenging, of not-knowing. Problem is expression and every expression is problematic. Therefore, metaphysical concepts are not "exact" concepts, not symbols, but disguised problems: freedom, force, will. It may happen that exact science transforms them into symbols, changing freedom into the symbolical indifference of choice-possibilities, force into the symbols of cause and effect, will into the symbols of motive and end. Their infinite and problematic expression, however, will be regained in the realm of metaphysics which guarantees the eternal continuity of seeking. Therefore, a metaphysical system is never comparable to an exact scientific system: The latter stands under the ideal of perfection, of perfect usefulness and finality. It is therefore absolute in the sense of exclusive. It is, however, absolute and exclusive only as long as it satisfies the end, as long as it serves as a working hypothesis. It has to be replaced by another system when it becomes unsatisfactory, imperfect, and useless for the purpose. The metaphysical system is never exclusive, never a whole in this sense, never perfect, and never merely useful. But it is an expression

[17] It is the Augustinian inheritance in Bonaventura which makes him base the divine creative knowledge on the lively concept of "expressio." And always again he challenges the old concept of "similarity" and dissolves it and questions it as a similitudo which is rather a dissimilitudo, which has nothing of "participation" or "imitation," but is a "similitudo extra genus," grown out of a dynamic "intentio veritatis." (I. *Sent.* d. 35 a. 1 qu. 1 and 2.)

of the eternal and infinite inquiry, and as an expression of eternal problems it is eternal itself.

Identity, analogy, and symbolism are three attempts to usurp and transform the infinite into the ideal of perfection and finality. Identity prevails in the ancient thought, analogy in scholasticism, and symbolism in our modern time. There is in this historic development a growing resignation: the Greek philosophy believed that it grasped and held the divine in the identity of its thought; scholasticism separated the spheres of heaven and earth and bridged the gap only by the narrow path of analogy; modern thought builds a world of symbols, indulges in science, and is resigned to stating that science has to substitute and to make good for the lost knowledge of the divine.

III

It is easy to understand that the revolution against the rule of perfection and finality did not restrict itself to the one sphere of human action, the aesthetic sphere. If the concept of divine perfection was wrong, then it was wrong everywhere where man reached above himself and believed he had traced the divine mark. Then it was wrong also in the realm of ethics.

Here again it was Kant who made an assault, the first serious assault, against perfection—and again he broke the power of this concept at its core: in the idea of end, of finality. Away from an ethics of ends, was his demand, and so he repeated what half a millennium before Master Eckhart had preached, asking for works without a "warumb."[18] The fulfillment of ends is only useful, never good. We cannot arrive at the good over utility, expediency—we may extend this utility as far as we want, even

[18] Master Eckhart: Edit. Pfeiffer, page 66, 5.

to a utility of the whole world. All ethics of ends has led to nothing but utilitarianism. And the English utilitarians are the most honest and most consistent representatives of the ethics of finality and perfection. Therefore their system is the most enlightening: Bentham transforms ethics into a mathematics of utility, into a pure calculation of expediency: the greatest utility for the greatest number, i.e. for all. Utility for all is perfection, complete, total utility and finality, human society as a total economic system. And it is not accidental that this total utility arose out of the old Epicurean ideal of individual utility. Individual or society—this distinction results here merely from the more or less vague decision as to where to limit the totality of end and utility. Self-realization of the individual or of society—the ideal is the same, and with rigor Kant attacks the so-called "self-perfection" which Christian Wolff taught as ethical ideal. Self-perfection is like all perfection an erroneous introduction of purpose into ethics.[19] It is only a disguise of the way in which self-perfection generally appears in the ethical systems: as realization of pleasure, as hedonism Hedonism—also in its finer forms of spiritual happiness —is the last consequence, the "summum bonum" of all ethics of ends and the ultimate interpretation of ethical perfection. Fulfillment of all ends; total, complete, perfect satisfaction of our wishes—this is the static ideal of Greek systematic rationalism.[20]

[19] Kant: *Critique of Prac. Reason* § 8 remark II.

[20] The most interesting modern attempt in this direction—done without compromise—is P. Weiss: *Reality*. The author tries to extend the Greek ideal of perfect completeness over all spheres of reality, even over ethics. When Weiss, however, states that this completeness and perfection are attainable only as an "abstract" and as a "vicarious" completeness, he seems to indicate that complete perfection is in fact limited to the rational sphere of systematization. Besides: the actual realization of

This rational ideal of perfect happiness, however, is a mere abstraction. An absolute fulfillment, a complete cessation of wishes, is lethargy and by no means happiness. In happiness—rightly understood—there is always want, desire, longing.[21] Satisfaction is only a phase, scarcely distinguishable, as the present is scarcely abstractable out of the flow of past into future. It is in all satisfaction that expectation remains and that regret is anticipated; happiness is, therefore, essentially transient, fugitive—unless it degenerates into an unhappy satiety.

It does not help to transplant happiness as perfect fulfillment into another life to come, an attempt in which rationalism generally takes refuge and which even Kant did not avoid. This part of Kant's ethics and religious philosophy is the result of his instinctive concessions and compromises with the utilitarian society of the eighteenth century. Just as he drove out of art the concept of end, but preserved it in the formula of "subjective purposiveness without purpose," so also he eliminated the end in ethics as the "matter" of action, but restored it again in his concept of a "formal lawfulness." His so-called "formal ethics" has in fact only a negative meaning: no material ethics, no ethics of ends. But, in order to give to this negative result a positive meaning, Kant turned to a rather complicated solution, to a law which is its own application, a law of lawfulness. In fact, he confesses that "how a law directly and of itself could be a determining principle of a will—that is an unsolvable problem and identical with the question: how a free will

this completeness would mean the end of life and all human values and be—even as an ideal—somehow unsatisfactory.

[21] Leibniz: *Nouv. Ess.* II, 21, § 36: "L'inquiétude est essentielle à la félicité des créatures, laquelle ne consiste jamais dans une parfaite possession, qui les rendrait insensible et comme stupide."

is possible."[22] So his empty law as end and motive means only that the will has no motive, no end besides itself; that it is the free, infinite will, unconditioned in its spontaneous simplicity. After having chosen this detour, however, and after having pushed the formal law, the empty lawfulness into the role of an end, all the old requisites of the ethics of ends found their way into his young and revolutionary system. Now it did not suffice any more to withdraw into the relation of identity, which always has to help out when philosophy is at the end of its rational interpretation. Now it was not enough to make the law its own application, man his own end and self-purpose, lawgiver identical with lawtaker—it was even necessary to proceed to an "ultimate end," not only of men, but of the whole creation.[23] And this ultimate end, as "summum bonum," appears in a strangely complicated relation to the moral law as worthiness for happiness in the other world. God becomes the guarantor of happiness, of perfect satisfaction and finality. So Kant states at last "the most exact conformity" between morality and happiness, and he mentions in this context—which is significant—the Biblical term "honor of God" and praises it as the "best expression." The "doxa," the wrong Greek translation of the living God,[24] is now for Kant the best expression of the infinite nature of the Divine. So Kant moves here again entirely in the field of the totally ordered cosmos, its proportions and laws, and of the rational knowledge of the perfect God who is the guarantor of final satisfaction and its happiness.

[22] Kant: *Critique of Pract. Reason*, chap. III (Motives of pure pract. Reason).

[23] Kant: *Critique of Pract. Reason*, chap. V (Dialectic).

[24] See page 27. Aquinas, too, is inclined to define as the goal of the world: "gloria Dei," δόξα θεοῦ. (*Summa Theol.* I, 65 a. 2.)

Here, however, we have to raise the following question: Is it really true that satisfaction, fulfillment of ends, plays the highest, even the exclusive, role in human life? Or is it not rather our intellectual endeavor to explain and to understand which makes us envisage merely those kinds of desire which can be closed into the rational relation of motive and end? If, as we saw before, even true happiness excludes the satisfaction of ends, how much more must this be so with regard to the deeper longings of the human soul?

To be sure, in a certain medium-sphere of our life the demands are determined by ends and find their conclusion in the fulfillment of these ends. The normal man— as the animal—wants satisfaction for his daily needs, and he desires for the sake of satisfaction. Even love, as far as animal-love is concerned, pure sexual love, is turned toward a definite end of satisfaction and dies away after satisfaction has been achieved. There is, however, not only this sexual love in men, but also a spiritual love which we call a higher one, because it is not consumed in ends and does not die in a satisfaction, but lives an infinite life beyond the world of ends or, as we may put it, beyond the grave.

When we said that our striving for ends corresponds to a medium-sphere of life, we meant that there are other spheres of life which rank before and behind this medium-sphere, and in which desire is not turned merely toward fulfillment. We overlook these spheres, because we have become accustomed to regard the normal social conduct of men as the only conduct possible. Before we reach, however, the balance of the socially active man, we are children or savages, and as such we usually do not load our desires with a realization of ends. We let these desires roam boundless and aimless in the infinite. This childish kind of desire we do not call a "willing," but a "wishing." The savage and the child wish, i.e. their desire is not tied to a realization by deeds and not confined to the possibilities of limited ends. Their wishes roam into the indefinite, impossible. The savage and the child dream—and many grown-up people, weak in willing, do this their life long. As far as such wishes are at all joined to fulfillments, the realization of them is not undertaken by the wisher but is left to more powerful beings, demons, fairies, Gods. These supernatural powers may give shape and reality to the infinity and indistinctness of the wish-dream.

The savage and the child wish the impossible. There is, however, a mature way of willing which neither remains in the childish stage of mere wishing nor is satisfied with the rational balance of the normal active man who limits his will to that which he has already experienced as truly possible. It is the man who, in a creative way, extends the sphere of the possible by his willing and so makes possible what until then had seemed impossible. He does not turn his eyes away from the world of realization, as the dreamer does, but takes into account the realm of possibilities in order to transcend it by the energy of his willing. Such a man does not start with a fixed and limited end, finding his satisfaction in a likewise limited fulfillment. It is an ideal which he lives but cannot put into words, and this ideal is constantly developing, taking new shape in the actions which lead to its realization and driving always beyond the scope of these actions. Therefore, only following generations are able to interpret and understand what has been done in this way.

This infinite urge is not unknown to the great thinkers of the past. It is the Augustinian idea of love, conceived now as the infinite search for truth, now as the creative will of men, and widened by St. Francis to an all-embracing bond which unifies the world and overcomes it. To "overcome" means in the tradition of St. Paul and St. Francis not a mere negation and turning away from the world, but on the contrary a thorough penetration, a passing through and a taking in, as it can be done only by those who go beyond. Who understands has always to go beyond. St. Francis was not a pantheist. A pantheist, like Thales of Miletus, reduces all things to a general denominator, water, and builds his complete and perfect system of the world on this principle of homogeneous and universal unification. But when St. Francis calls the sun, the moon, and the stars his brothers and sisters, he takes all things into the core of humanity, in order to detach them from their merely relative and fixed existence; and he sees them in the light in which men should be regarded in their drive beyond which we call love.[25]

Kant also was on the way to an ethics of love. His infinite will, not satisfied with the expediency of our ends, should have found love as its true meaning. But Kant, after having cleared away the perfection of ends, blocked his way by filling the empty space with the substitute constructions of self-goal and formal law. In the ethics of love, however, man is not a case of the application of a general law under which the ego meets the thou, so to speak, "per analogiam," and every one respects in his field of finality the other "as himself." A law of total

[25] In this way a new insight into nature was attained, and this new insight was fructified by the great Christian art which made nature not only the background of the religious drama, but even the direct expression of its most intensive urge. So Giotto, under Franciscan influence, laid the ground for the great nature and landscape painting of the following centuries.

validity, a law for all, as Kant demands it, belongs to science, but not to an ethics of love. It would mean even a relapse into the adoration of totality and "all," a concession to the ideal of completeness, to ask for "love of all men." As if the totality of men as an observable row were put before us and were an object of penetration. "All" exists only in abstract science, as species or genus. In life the individual exists alone. Who loves "all," loves nobody. To love every single individual, every thou we actually meet, is more than to love all. Love is not turned toward the totality of species but toward every individual in our reach.

The significance of "law" should therefore not be overestimated in the field of ethics. This overestimation again has its basis in the ideal of perfection, of total completeness in a limited system. Even in science such a lawful systematization is attainable only in a hypothetical way. Our scientific necessity is necessary only with regard to an underlying principle and under the hypothetical supposition of its validity. This may satisfy us here to such an extent that we are even allowed to forget the hypothetical nature of our law and to claim its unrestricted validity as long as we have no better hypothesis. We have a practical right to treat our hypothetical necessity as categorical as long as it satisfies our needs.

But in the sphere of human life and value this does not hold. Here we should never forget that every system of rules is carried by ends and that even a so-called ultimate end is only a limited end. We may fulfill this end in a perfect way, in a complete way, but in doing so we adjust ourselves only to a more or less hypothetical perspective, a limited, and in its limitation accidental, perspective, as it turns up in the course of history, relative to the needs and wants of the time.

Such a relative attitude, in spite of its perfect fulfill-ment and the resulting good conscience, falls short with regard to the fact that man knows himself as absolute. Man cannot stop at a relative position. And so it happens that the incompatibility of a merely relative law and the necessity of an absolute standard compels men to treat the relative law as if it were absolute. Philosophy, however, has to go deeper. It has to reduce the laws in the field of religion, ethics, and aesthetics to that which they really are and which can perhaps be compared best to what we call "rituals." This means that it is useful and even necessary that the way to the divine, the good, and the beautiful leads over a system of purposive and com-plete rules, that such rules always will be, because in these realms ends will always be set and fulfilled in order to organize the life and mutual understanding of a group. But these ends and their system of rules never fully ex-plain and exhaust the drive in religion, ethics, and aesthetics. That there are rules may be necessary, but how they are is accidental, relative, and changing in the course of time. They are, like all systems of perfection and completeness, merely exclusive, never absolute.

The danger, however, and the fatal error is that the ideal of perfection is not satisfied with the exclusiveness of the system of laws: it wants its absoluteness. And so in the field of art the rules of the schools, in the field of ethics the morals of classes, castes, and professions, in the field of religion the dogmas of the sects have caused ritual battles and persecutions. Every school has claimed its rules as the only truth, every class and caste its ethics as the only way to purity, every religious sect its dogma as the only path to salvation—and ruthlessly they have tried to wipe out and extinguish every other one which stood in their way to victory.

Here, more than anywhere else, the idol of "absolute perfection" revealed its limited and erroneous nature. The result was desperation and skepticism. The relativity of the good, the holy, and the beautiful seemed the only possible way out for those who did not understand that it was only the system of purposive laws which had broken down and had shown itself to be merely relative.

Whenever the principle of perfection dominates in ethics there is a tendency to dissolve ethics into state-law. Plato is here the outstanding example. The good as a system of rules under an organizing purpose is the order of the state-law. And so it cannot astonish us that Plato praises justice as the highest ethical value. Justice is order, it is the observance of a certain place in the system. Legal "duty," therefore, is the meaning of this ethics, and the essence of such a duty is limitation, a narrow observance of a boundary line, the exact keeping of a neatly defined position in a systematic whole which is an end in itself and therefore perfection. From this identification of state-law and ethics, moral duties have assumed a tendency to group together with other duties in a firmly established, clearly defined order of rank and gradation. But wherever there is a hierarchy of duties, with all its pitfalls of a "scale of values" and "conflicts of values," there has to be arbitrariness in the achievement of a perfect order. Contingency and violence of decision will work together to justify the "perfect order" by some all-embracing end which cannot prove its birthright and therefore will have to be hidden or disguised. In vain Kant tried to save the idea of law and end by widening them to such an extent that law and end were emptied to a mere form without content: self-goal and law of lawfulness. In doing this Kant lost every possibility of guiding men in their doings, although he protected them perhaps against the narrow pride of a perfect ethical fulfillment.

For ethical perfection is a danger to men: not only because it turns, as we have seen, man against man in his claim for an absolute possession of the good, but also because it develops an unbearable pride in the members of every ethical clan. Whoever belongs to such a group and possesses the perfect system of rules can in fulfilling these rules be a "perfectly good" person and enjoy thoroughly his own perfection. In fulfilling the law and every letter of the law he will be the "righteous" man, the just, the pharisee, he will be the one whom the Gospel despises and compares unfavorably to the penitent sinner,[26] he will be the ethical perfectionist, the virtuoso of virtue, the man without defects, self-sure and proud of himself.

Only when men feel that the fulfillment of their moral laws alone does not suffice, then all these rituals, these duties may become meaningful through their drive beyond, through love. Love alone changes the merely relative value of duty and law into an absolute one. Love itself is not a fixed duty, not an end which waits for its fulfillment. If it were an end, it would vanish in a fulfillment as all ends do. But love is the source of duties and as such maintains itself beyond all fulfillment, giving rise to always new duties. Therefore, the lover never sees the beloved in a fixed position, never holds him in any of the disguises which our ends and their fulfillment force us to adopt, never fixes him in his occasional profession or present state of character, where the unloving alone sees him. Love sees always beyond, is always on the way to more and better. Love surely is blind, but only for the fixation which means so much to practical society.

[26] Luke 5: 32 and 15: 7.

For love is indeed seeing in regard to the force and possibility in the beloved which is a force and possibility to overcome the fixation with all its deficiency. Love, and nothing but love, educates. It educates in driving ahead beyond the present stage. In order to do so, it will have to acknowledge ends and the fulfillment of ends, duties, and their order. No love, however, is true, if it does not feel in each fulfillment of ends and in every stage of development that which is beyond all ends, duties, and fulfillments, and if it does not readily sacrifice the ambition of achievement, the pride of success for that which can never be achieved by ends: the personality as such who lives and is loved beyond and above all its ends.

What we call "sacrifice" has its vital and true place in ethics. It is a readiness to reach beyond the limited ends, successes, and stages of education unto something to which all these duties are only subservient. Surely it is not our bad nature which has to be sacrificed for a duty, as Kant taught, but rather our good nature which leads over the way of confirmation and trial to a surrender, and that which has to be surrendered is good because it is a part of the way to the good. We love that which we sacrifice. This truth is at the root of the holy myths of divine sacrifice, as we find them in the creed of all people and all times.

Sacrifice is a surrender of ends for something which is no end and no fulfillment. It is not an abandonment of a value for a higher one. Such definition would be that of any business transaction, where expenses are incurred for the sake of higher profit—and indeed sacrifice has often in history degenerated into a business transaction. What gives its unique character to sacrifice is that a finite value is given for an infinite one; an end for something which transcends the sphere of ends; a perfection for something which no longer fits into the category of perfect or imperfect. It is, therefore, even inadequate to say: a sacrifice was made "for" something, "for the sake" of something. This again would transform sacrifice into a means for an end. What appears—seen from the world of ends, of fixed levels and achievements—as a sacrifice, is for the will only a way of freedom and openness, a kind of readiness and willingness. This readiness and willingness is not an action which goes along with the other actions, it is a willingness which beside all active work of love, its educating power and untiring endeavor to advance the possibilities in the life of the beloved, accompanies the various phases of action as an unchanging ground of existence.

It is this ground of existence, this readiness of sacrifice, which gives to all our doings a new meaning and fuses them into a flux in which they lose their fixed and limited character and become a part of our life under the unifying idea of SERVICE. Service is the unity of love in which the single deeds and duties lose their self-importance, perfection, and purposive seclusion and count merely as stages and phases of a life of service. Service is not an "achievement," a fulfillment of an end, a usefulness. It is surrender, as sacrifice is surrender, not for the sake of some finite task, but for the beyond of all tasks, for an infinity of life, for a will, a personality. One may speak of "serving a task, an idea," but then behind task and idea must be something which is more than task and idea, something which cannot be put into words, but can only be lived. In fact, service is a surrender and devotion to a will, and Master Eckhart may have meant something similar when he demanded works, but above all works and as beyond works, he praised the "inner work" which is will and personality.[27] Although achievable only in outward works, it nevertheless transcends these works and the satisfaction of their fulfillment.

The idea of service found its way into the daily life of men, lifted this life above mere expediency and conveyed an ethical value to labor. The Bible already sanctifies labor: "The sleep of a laboring man is sweet"; "work with your own hands as we commanded you"; "if any would not work, neither should he eat."[28] Throughout the Middle Ages religious orders regarded themselves as an army of laborers whose rules commanded work,[29] and it was only the continuation of this idea that in the time of the Reformation under Lutheran[30] and Puritan[31] influence labor assumed as a "calling," as a "vocation," the character of a religious service and gave a new dignity to men.

It was inevitable that the idea of service, entering the sphere of daily life, should not always keep clear of the idol of perfect mechanization and that it should sometimes wither into the fulfillment of a fixed and well rounded function, ending at last in the pedantry of bureaucratism. Such a mechanization of service may have its value in society, but it is a danger in the realm of ethics, where the sphere of action is not accurately rounded out with neatly defined ends and duties. Service

[27] Master Eckhart (Edit. Pfeiffer), page 434, 1; see also page 353, 3.

[28] Eccles. 5: 12; I Thess. 4: 11; II Thess. 3: 10. Compare the opposite view as expressed in some Greek writers: Hesiodus (*Works and Days* 42) complains that men cannot achieve in one day's labor enough profit to live for a whole year; or Aristotle who calls labor ignoble and excludes the working men from political life (*Pol.* VII, 8).

[29] See the "First Rule" of St. Francis and his *Testament*.

[30] Luther (*Erl. ausg.* 10, page 233): "Jeder ist in irgendeinen Beruf berufen"; in the same way already the Mystic Joh. Tauler (Ed. Vetter no. 42).

[31] Baxter: *Christian Directory* I. ch. x.

and freedom belong together, as they do in the teaching of Rousseau and Kant. Laws and duties are in bondage as long as they do not receive their meaning from service. Service alone softens the rigor and inflexibility which result necessarily from the generalization of the law. It is the spirit of service which rejuvenates decaying laws. Service does not free men *from* the law, but it makes them free in handling, interpreting, and applying the law. The more a man is under the power of service, the freer he is in the mastery of the law. It is the spirit of the law which he lives, not the perfect wording and exact letter as it stands. This may be the meaning of St. Paul's teaching that love and its service are above the law.

The law is known. Socrates' ethics knows the law and teaches the law as the good. The true ethics, however, cannot be taught and learned, but grows through the loving service and understanding of a person. This is what we call following an example. The example educates. Therefore, in the life of every child the moment comes when the mere: "you shall" or "you shall not" of the authoritative law loses its effect, and love to parents, teachers, friends takes the lead in the further education. But even in this stage of a living service the ideal of perfection may become a danger and may degenerate the service into a kind of routine. As in art the wish for imitation grew out of the idol of perfection, producing perfect illusion and thus falsifying art,[32] so also here in ethics imitation, the perfect copying of the model, becomes an easy means for self-satisfaction. Imitation of a model may be excused and may even be helpful on the lowest stage of life, as a childish beginning. But if the child does not free itself in time, imitation draws it downwards, instead of upwards. Imitation makes those

[32] See page 65.

90

who imitate as well as those who are imitated a laughing stock, and it has always been an efficient instrument in comedies. The more "perfect" imitation is, the more it kills life and degrades. The true way of following is not imitation, it is freedom, because it gives birth to new values, new duties and is creative in every moment of its service. It permanently extends the framework of duties, never commanding a particular deed to be done, but rather leaving it to the follower to decide the scope and volume of his virtue. To put it in a paradoxical way: The ethics of service makes it the duty of man, not only to do his duty, but to do more.

This idea of service in which men freely follow an example is the driving force in HISTORY. It is this and just this which makes history. The history of an individual person as well as the history of mankind is formed by the idea of service. Therefore historiography is not an "exact science," not a perfect context of lawful relations, but an insight into the idea of service as it lives in a certain time and in a certain people. Even the concept of a "people" as a historic entity has grown out of the idea of service. Therefore, the first great and consistent historiography is that of the Bible, where a people is shown united and carried away by the prophetic idea of service. And this idea of a spiritual unity, called the "people," had to be reborn in the medieval religious struggle between council, pope, and king. With the right understanding for that which made this unity of the people, the greatest thinkers of that time conceive the spiritual unity of the people as "instrumentum Dei."[33] Born out of the idea of

[33] John of Paris: *De Pot. Reg. et Pap.* c. II and 16; Marsil. Padov: *Defensor Pacis* I c. 9; William of Ockham: *Dial.* III tr. 2, l. I c. 27; Cusanus: *Concord. Cathol*: II, 19; III praef. and c. 4.

service the people assumed the character of holiness which in the process of time gave way to the idea of "sovereignty of the people," and from that time on the history of democracy is a history of freedom. But freedom, sovereignty of the people means in the light of history: freedom for service.

Not always does the model of service stand clearly outlined before the eyes of the people. Often it may be realized in the person of God or of a prophetic man; often it may only in a dim way be present to the time as an ideal of living, conceived by the best, preached and lived as a responsibility, as the calling of the time, as its vocation and task. The historian has to search for this ideal, to understand and to interpret it, in order to grasp the true meaning of a time. What we call "progress in history" is the persistent approach toward this ideal which ever clearer and stronger realizes itself in the thoughts and doings of a time and provides the people with a growing knowledge of themselves and a growing freedom of action. It is the striving for such an ideal of life, for a new task, for a new dignity of man, for a new service which makes history to us more vital than it has ever been since the revolutions of the eighteenth century.

The Greek people, not less than any other people in history, have lived their idea of service. But their interpreters of history, deceived by their ideal of perfection, have misunderstood the true meaning of historiography. Thucydides states clearly[34] that his writing of history has the purpose of collecting material, from which general rules of political conduct may be learned for future use. Here "history" indeed is that for which the term "ἱστορία" was invented: a natural history, a description of natural

[34] Thucydides: *Pelop. War.* I, 22.

and general facts which serves as an example for the universal laws of events, for the scientific systematization of politics. Such a political system was the ultimate end of historiography, in order to perfect the political conduct. The ideal of technical perfection is here again the Greek goal—and it is only a short step from this ideal of technical perfection in world-conduct to its hypostasis in the divine mind: to God's perfect and total and complete "providence." Providence, however, and perfection are restricted to the very limited and inferior sphere of human ends, and are both surpassed and carried beyond themselves by the true ideal of history: the ideal of service.

The Greek identification of ethics and state-law has here its parallel in the identification of history and politics, both under the spell of the idol of perfection. In fact, history is always much more, it is the history of civilization, and political history represents only a part of the history of civilization. The part which political history plays is that part which more than any other is in constant danger of surrendering to the idol of perfection and so of declining into stagnation. Political states tend toward technical and mechanical perfection, toward self-sufficiency, seclusion, and totality, and so often lose their contact with the life and development of their people.[35] Therefore, it can happen that a state degenerates as a political unity and nevertheless, at the same time, its people contribute highly to the civilization of mankind. It can even happen that the people free themselves from their political decay and become politically rejuvenated

[35] Toynbee: *A Study of History* (Vol. IV, 119, 261, 303 and Vol. IV, 321) states as symptoms of decay just those qualities which we have met as tendencies toward perfection: imitation, idolatry, standardization, mechanization, universal states (totalities), etc.

through their spiritual resources. An historian who judges a people mainly according to their political standard will be unfair and unjust, because in this field fixation, idolatry, and mechanization will often blur the picture. The true historian will find his way into the service and future of a people, untrammeled by the errors and deviations which occasionally occur in their life. An historian is somehow a prophet; prophecy means a profound understanding of tradition and of the way to the future which grows out of the living past.

This future is never closed, neither in the life of the individual nor in that of a people. "Individual" and "people" are not totalities, walled up in birth and death. This merely biological interpretation of history, as we find it in Oswald Spengler,[36] is again an offspring of the scientific ideal of perfect completeness and results in secluded bodies of civilization without mutual contact and understanding. What refutes and contradicts this interpretation, which would portray history as a nonsensical repetition of beginnings and endings, is the people's and the individual's belief in immortality, i.e. in an always open future of service. Service, grounded in personality, knows neither birth nor death and lives a life of infinite enrichment. In this life the ideal grows and transforms itself permanently and with it the possibilities of its followers. New generations enter into the service, new people continue what older people began, impressed and imbued with the spirit of their ancestors. This is what we call "continuity" in history, and this is what guarantees the permanent progress, a progress which does not presume a definite, perfect, and total plan which, earlier or later, would be fulfilled and would end prog-

[36] Spengler: *Decline of the West*, Vol. I, ch. 2, nr. 6-8.

ress and stop development. Immortality, in the individual and in the people, is the transcendence of service which reaches beyond their own limits of life and makes possible a continuous giving and taking, understanding and devotion throughout the generations of men.

There is no sense in trying to define this service and its ideal as the "true meaning of world history," in calling it, for instance, the "growing self-confidence of men" or the "increasing freedom." "Self" and "freedom" are only approximate interpretations of a much broader service, in the course of which that which we call "self" and "freedom" change their meanings. "World," at last, is only the sum of the deposits and residues which the eternally changing movement of service leaves behind, and which keeps on living as the "past" in the annals of history. Should service as the testimony of the future end, this "world" of the past would all at once, as a meaningless waste, become the totality and perfect completeness of an entirely terminated past.

In fact, however, history is never really past, it is always a present stimulation to service.[37] The world, as an historical unity, is that which has served and in serving has set the task for the future; it is like every sacrifice living on in that for which it has been offered. The world is the ground and readiness and stimulation for future service. Nothing repeats itself in the history of service, least of all the world of the past as Thucydides thought; but as a living tradition the past world is the stepping-stone for our freedom and openness toward the future.

Wherever the idea of perfection emerges and starts to shape the world-view of men, we may be sure that the

[37] See Kierkegaard, *Philosoph. Fragments,* chap. IV, interlude.

rational concept of end, of purpose is at work. Reality here is finality, and so being and perfection were identified in the Greek and post-Greek rationalism. Whether one made God the end, as did Aristotle, or whether one made our own self the goal of perfection, as some idealists tried, for our problem this difference is not important: the one degraded God to a scientific system, the other mechanized men. In neither of these cases are the contradictions avoidable which grow out of the hypostasis of the end, the various paradoxes which we found in the course of this work: the absoluteness of relation, the infinity of the finite, the first cause, the unmoved mover, the empty law of lawfulness, the self-goal, etc. What we do not deny is the fact Kant stated: that totality is behind all purposeful action, whether it have its cause in an impulse of human nature, or whether it be regarded as an objective order. But what we do deny is the assumption that this totality, this completeness is the ever striven for divine nature itself. The ideas of completeness, of totality, of end and perfection receive their justification in a limited field, and they receive this justification as a limitation by that which is beyond them and therefore is apt to draw the limits. The whole of systematic relations and perfection is not to be omitted, and neither is our drive toward it, which we call rational knowledge. But all rational knowledge is overlapped and embraced by a wider knowledge of a beyond which we touch in the idea of an inner force, of will and personality. This knowledge we usually do not call "knowledge," because it is not constructed by the mediation of inference and does not become conscious in the completeness and balance of a judgment. We call this knowledge because of its immediacy FAITH. Faith is that kind of knowledge which knows the force, the will, the personality. Wherever personality is, faith is. We believe in ourselves and we believe in the personality of our fellowmen. Man's experience of man is always faith. Surely, in the mechanism of daily life, where men are treated not only as personalities, but more often as objects, as ends or means to ends, our knowledge of these living objects is mediated; it is the rational expedient knowledge which the test procures. But no testing ever penetrates into the personality of men which we know only by faith, by confidence. Confidence is deeper than testing. Confidence and faith alone give us the certainty of inner life, of will, of personality and its readiness for devotion and love.

Faith and knowledge are not two grades of the same approach, they are entirely different: knowledge as the mastery of things, ends, perfection, and systematization; faith as the penetration into the person, into the beyond of life. Faith is not an "intuitive" knowledge, not a knowledge of identity, as the Greek thought who conceived "immediacy" in the rational and perfect relation of an identical judgment.[38] Faith is not identity: In faith the difference and distance between the faithful one and the person of his devotion are inextinguishably preserved. Faith is a way; distance belongs to the way, and with it the possibility of error and doubt. Therefore, the prophet receives the revelation of the divine in the distress of his heart, in the remoteness of his limited and doubting self. This is why St. Augustine saw in doubt and only in doubt the ground for certainty and why St. Paul found "fear and trembling" at the root of faith. The religious fear is a fear of being lost, and this fear is never quite extinguished in the hearts of believers. Those who, like

[38] See page 38.

Hobbes and Hume,[39] see in fear the source of religion, should know that this fear of primitive men, this fear of being lost, is the dim divination of a salvation and that the "early religions of fear" which we stigmatize as mere superstitions represent the first endeavors to find the way out of fear and desperation to confidence and salvation. Our religions, the mature religions of confidence, therefore, had to develop out of that genuine fear of losing salvation; and by strengthening the trust which had dimly been felt in this fear, very slowly fear was overcome by confidence. Even in our mature religions, however, fear, as the expression of distance and of the possibility of error, has its place and has maintained its importance in the feeling of awe. Awe measures the distance between the faithful man and his God, while love overbridges this distance and becomes the living force of education.

And this drama of faith repeats itself wherever man believes in man. Here also love, as the way of following and approaching the beloved model, will never quite blot out the distance, the seclusion in the beloved which keeps awake reverence and respect. Never in the relation of man to man is an exact, total, and perfect knowledge of identity achieved, but always only "belief," a belief which preserves and enhances a remoteness, never quite overcome, and makes it necessary that men who love have to believe in each other, have to trust each other, and to take for granted what they never exactly know.

The conflict of millennia between knowledge and faith —this conflict which raged especially throughout the Middle Ages—is a conflict between the pantheism of the Greek world-order and the living God of creation. It was a misunderstanding and a narrowing of the faith, when

[39] Hobbes: *Leviathan*, chap. 6, 11, 12. Hume: *Nat. Hist. of Relig.*, sect. 13.

faith was limited to the written revelation of a divine book. Faith surely is always faith in a revelation, i.e. in an active, living source. But this source is not the word, not the mere concept—it is the person, its will and creative love. In this sense faith can exist only in revealed religions, only as faith in a personal God. A pure pantheistic order cannot be believed, it has to be known. This pure pantheism would, if it really ever existed, be limited to the totality and perfection of a scientific system. In fact, religion was always more than that, because even the most intellectual man has an inkling of his rational limitation, of the contradictions and unsolvable problems which perfection and purpose lay upon our mind.

Therefore behind all—even the pantheistic—religions stands more or less clouded the person of God. And it has been since its beginning the noblest task of philosophy to seek beyond science the unity between knowledge of ends and belief in personality. Out of this problem and its necessity philosophy is born, as a drive toward unity of faith and knowledge. Perhaps it originated in Greece, because knowledge for the first time had to conquer its place at the side of the overwhelming faith of the Orient. Just as well, however, philosophy can become necessary—and so it is in later centuries—when faith in its turn has to defend its life against an extending knowledge. This was the task of philosophy in St. Augustine's time, in the early Middle Ages and again in the eighteenth century of Leibniz and Kant.

As long as faith and knowledge stand their ground together, philosophy will be necessary—not to separate these realms, as was done in the late Scholastic period and in the Renaissance, but to unite them with each other and to reveal the sphere of their innermost contact.

This contact makes it indispensable to reduce to its

limits an idea which has been born in the course of history and in the struggle between science and faith: the idea of "absolute perfection." This idea had its time when a young science had to be protected against religion. But it cannot stand the test of an impartial philosophical judgment, before which it is forced to give up the pretension of being more than a limited human finality.

INDEX

Absolute, 33ff
Albertus Magnus, 41
All, *see* Totality
Analogy, 41, 72, 76
Anaxagoras, 21
Anselm, 21, 24, 38, 43
Antinomy, 35
Aristotle, 8, 16, 18, 19, 21, 23, 30, 34, 35, 37, 38, 45, 47, 50, 55, 65
Art, 58ff
Athanasius, 74
Augustine, 31, 39ff, 43, 45, 52, 56, 75, 97, 99

Baxter, 89
Beauty, 60, 70
Bergson, 43, 50
Bible, 25ff
Bonaventura, 40, 45, 49, 54, 75
Burke, 60

Completeness, 9, 15ff, 37, 96
Creation, 35, 53, 66
Cusanus, 4, 24, 43, 48, 52, 54, 91

Democritus, 3, 5
Descartes, II, 13, 21, 24, 34, 37, 41, 42, 50
Dionysios, 24, 30, 40, 44, 45, 46, 49, 54
Doxa, 27, 79
Duns Scotus, 37, 38, 40, 52, 54
Duty, 86

Empedocles, 38, 53
End, *see* Purpose
Entelechy, 18
Epicurus, 36
Ethics, 76ff
Excellence, 30
Expression, 69ff

Faith, 96
Force, 26, 51ff
Francis, Saint, 82, 89
Freedom, 35, 52, 92, 95

God, 19ff, 26ff, 36ff, 42, 55, 57, 98, 99

Hartshorne, 32
Hegel, 20, 31ff, 40, 46
Heraclitus, 18, 21, 70
History, 91ff
Hobbes, 98
Humanity, 73, 91, 94
Hume, 98
Hypothesis, 6, 75, 83

Identity, 23, 34, 38, 76
Imitation, 65, 90
Individual, 36, 73, 83, 94
Infinity, 39ff
Intuition, 38

Kant, 8, 10, 24, 34, 35, 50, 51, 52, 60ff, 76ff, 82, 85, 87, 96, 99
Kierkegaard, 95

Language, 71
Law, 78, 83, 85
Leibniz, 13, 24, 34, 37, 42, 52, 55, 71, 78, 99
Limitation, 16
Love, 80, 83
Luther, 89

Maimonides, 29, 45, 54
Marsilius, 91
Master Eckhart, 4, 40, 45, 46, 54, 57, 76, 88
Matter, 18, 19, 37, 52
Metaphysics, 75

INDEX